MW00912326

WHEN
HURT
HAPPENS

CR boomt

DEALING WITH LIFE
WHEN
HURT
HAPPENS

C.R. Boonstra

TATE PUBLISHING & *Enterprises*

Dealing with Life when Hurt Happens
Copyright © 2011 by C.R. Boonstra. All rights reserved.

No part of this publication may be reproduced, stored in a retrieval system or transmitted in any way by any means, electronic, mechanical, photocopy, recording or otherwise without the prior permission of the author except as provided by USA copyright law.

Scriptures taken from the *Holy Bible, New International Version*®, NIV®. Copyright © 1973, 1978, 1984 by Biblica, Inc.™ Used by permission of Zondervan. All rights reserved worldwide. www.zondervan.com

The opinions expressed by the author are not necessarily those of Tate Publishing, LLC.

Published by Tate Publishing & Enterprises, LLC
127 E. Trade Center Terrace | Mustang, Oklahoma 73064 USA
1.888.361.9473 | www.tatepublishing.com

Tate Publishing is committed to excellence in the publishing industry. The company reflects the philosophy established by the founders, based on Psalm 68:11,
"The Lord gave the word and great was the company of those who published it."

Book design copyright © 2011 by Tate Publishing, LLC. All rights reserved.
Cover design by Christina Hicks
Interior design by Nathan Harmony

Published in the United States of America

ISBN: 978-1-61346-325-3
1. Religion / Christian Life / Personal Growth
2. Self-Help / Depression
11.07.11

Dedication

This book is dedicated first and foremost to my Savior, Jesus Christ, and then to all the people who have or are dealing with the negative things to which this challenging and non-respective world they live in subjects them.

Table of Contents

Prologue

Life is fragile. It cannot be put on hold but must be lived despite its susceptibility to malfunction and disappointment. We only get one, and by the time we figure out what we want to do with it, it's over.

Regardless of how, where, or when we live, things don't always go as planned. When the bottom falls out or something unexpected happens, we go from denial to acceptance, only to realize we don't know what to expect or do. Our natural instinct is survival—to hang on or just get through while trying to maintain dignity and normalcy.

Anybody that has endured anything from a small disappointment to a major setback knows how emotions, needs, relationships and choices, affect not only the end result, but our ability to cope with the process of getting there. When unplanned or unexpected things happen, our lives must change. Most of us don't embrace this kind of change because, not only are we unprepared, but it's usually not on our terms.

Although we try putting problems into a box to make things work in a uniform fashion, it rarely happens so easily. We are all unique in our personalities, emotions, priorities, and abilities, plus we have the added influence of our environment, culture, age, gender, and convictions.

Once we get past the pride and seek wisdom from those who have already endured and learned, we usually find not only common ground of a particular situation, but also a bond of understanding. Life is about relationships and maturity; it is a journey that comes in the form of many changes, choices, and the time that we are allowed to make an impact on those around us.

It is neither wrong nor shameful to seek help to improve life. It matters not what has contributed to where you are now. What matters is that you make the choice to move on in life.

Somewhere in our subconscious, we have gotten the idea we need to suppress, or ignore certain feelings and emotions that come during times of difficulty. Wrong. These human expressions are ways of dealing with life. It does not mean you're weak; it means you're normal.

What Is Happening?

Worried due to the circumstance you feel unjustly subjected to? Is fear of the unknown wrapping you in a blanket of more questions than answers? You probably feel alone, humiliated, unprepared, inadequate, judged by others, and challenged beyond your abilities.

Life can be overwhelming when it seems everything goes wrong or works against us. We may even feel cheated because of the abilities or resources we have compared to those around us. Our idea or plan of what life should be fails, and we find ourselves depending on others. If we are not self-sufficient and able to function normally in society, we tend to downgrade ourselves to the point of feeling useless. We become convinced that life as an unproductive person is too difficult, and that we have become nothing less than a burden to those around us.

It has been said that everybody has a story to tell, but it seems hard to find anybody that really cares to listen, or come along beside us for support when our burdens overwhelm.

As soon as I tell you it need not be that way, you will probably mentally flip the off switch, sarcastically saying to yourself, *What does this guy know? He has no idea what I've been dealing with; he's not living my life. How can he relate to my circumstance?*

First, I must tell you, I was right where you are. I could not write this if I did not experience the exact things I just described. As I write this, I am still in the middle of the trial God has allowed in my life. At this time I do not see a way for this to end in a good or timely manner from my limited human point of view.

I am not a person of credentials and book knowledge telling you what the practical answer is. It is only by personally going through the experience of having my own comfortable world go awry, that I hope to encourage and help you understand the emotional rollercoaster of unknowns and unwanted problems that *you* are personally subjected to.

Correct—I do not know your circumstance, but I do know we are all the same. It doesn't matter if we are of a certain ethnic background, man, woman, rich, poor, or any other quality that may define who we are. We were all created by God, are born, breathe air, have red blood, and eventually will die. We all have the same basic needs in life: To love or be loved, hope in something, and feel we have purpose. These all are forms of fulfillment that drive mankind.

Life isn't an always-sunshine, never-a-negative-moment, everything-is-easy fairytale. Without a doubt, we will all face times of uncertainty, difficult challenges, and the need to deal with changes we never intended to. It is during these times we feel the hurts of life.

Most of us are unprepared, and quickly come to the point of desperately wanting someone to give us comfort, through words of encouragement or a shoulder to lean on.

Depending on your personality and maturity, the potholes of life can and will, affect you differently than it may others. Additional contributing factors of influence can be age, health, environment, and those close to you.

I believe there are four basic categories of our makeup that leave us venerable to what can be called a hurt in life. We are not exempt from having to endure more than one, sometimes at the same time, and sometimes multiple times. The four types are:

1. Physical

2. Financial

3. Emotional

4. Spiritual

We will look at each of these areas from their own perspective in the following chapters. However, it is also vital to keep in mind how intertwined each of these categories are to the other, while we examine their particular role during life's difficulties.

So who exactly are these hurting people and what do they experience when life seems to have treated them unfairly? I suggest hurting people are those whose plans have been altered without their consent, forcing them to allow some unsolicited circumstance to be part of their life.

Hurting people sometimes feel they are in a prison, locked in a world that others cannot penetrate or relate to. Something came into their life, shattering what was once a calm, comfortable, satisfactory way of living, and feel set aside from the normal routines. As outsiders who want desperately to turn back time and return to the familiar ways of the past, initially they tell themselves, *It can't be happening; these things only happen to other people. I don't deserve this; I'm a good person.* Eventually we must acknowledge and accept the fact that whatever is happening must now be dealt with. We can't go back or ignore what has taken place, so once reality has set in, we must make personal choices and adjustments in our lives to include the changes.

When our ship finally comes in, we find ourselves at the airport—isn't that how life goes? We always seem to be in the wrong place at the wrong time. Things don't happen as we think they should, and we feel life has somehow treated us unfairly, especially when we did everything right and should be rewarded instead of penalized.

All that having been said, let me tell you there is hope! Our creator, God, cares for you as an individual. Yes, *you.* Each one of us is important to God. I will show you what I have learned and hopefully encourage you in your pursuit of living a life worth the effort.

Before you pass judgment on where I am heading or think I'm going to give the expected answers like *Think positive, and everything will work out,* I wish to tell you from my own experience that when things go sour, and life is out of balance, we fall down and it hurts. Getting back up takes time, effort, and sometimes help.

I must make one thing perfectly clear. I believe the Bible (God's word) is not only a guidebook, but also the final authority pertaining to what choices we should make concerning the struggles we may have throughout life. I will also inject a disclaimer by saying that when things are upside down, or confusing, the front door of having a perfect answer that fits every situation is absurd. A backdoor approach with the same result is sometimes necessary, always with a goal of restoring individual lives and relationships, to understanding, acceptance and contentment.

When things go wrong or different than what we consider logical or right, we begin to self-judge, allowing thoughts of worthlessness and self-pity to creep in. We need to stop beating ourselves up in this manner before we actually start believing it. Desiring improvement of circumstance to make our lives better is *not* wrong.

Regardless of what the hurt is, because you are the one directly involved it is the worst possible situation. The degree of difficulty or hurt, is directly related to how involved *you* as an individual are.

Sometimes in our frustration, we need someone to put our feelings into the right words. You may know the feelings but are unable to express them to the ones closest to you. We all need help at times, maybe due to lack of knowledge, misunderstanding, or even exhaustion from the events that have taken place. May this book be the aid, or insight you have longed to find, bridging the gap between feelings, communication, and helping others understand your pain. May it also help you connect with those involved in your life, as it exposes some of the underlying reasons we react as we do in uncharted, unwanted, life-altering circumstances.

Do you really believe there is a God? Without having some superior being to guide your life, are you at the mercy of chance? Is there purpose, reason, or even a future to look forward to? You are an intelligent human, one who has the ability to think, reason, and make choices. If you do not know God personally, I challenge you to ask yourself why.

Ecclesiastes is a book of the Bible written by Solomon, the wisest man who ever lived. He elaborates on the themes of how short and senseless life can be, how everything is the same from generation to generation, and how things don't always happen in the logical way we think they should. Job 14:1 sums up man's life on this earth. "Man born of woman, is of few days and full of trouble." The old saying, "The more things change, the more they stay the same," is dripping with truth. The simple application is that we are no different than anybody who has lived before us. So hang in there, persevere, continue on, keep your eye on the goal (living for God), and don't ever give up! God is in control and has a plan for you, even when things have a bleak outlook.

This book is not just for the hurting. It is also for those who genuinely desire to understand and be a support to those going through difficult situations in life.

Hurting is very real, but sometimes people hide it so others cannot see. Most people who hurt withdraw from telling even those close to them how they really feel, possibly for fear of being misunderstood, or for fear of being judged. Humans are proud and generally don't want to expose themselves as ones who may be weak enough to need the help or the support of others.

When someone is hurt physically, they go to the doctor or hospital to get the necessary help. Depending on the severity of the wound or infliction, is the amount of time and type of treatment or medicine required for proper healing. When people hurt in non-physical ways due to life bringing undesirable situations, they too need time and the right type of treatment to heal and recover. We cannot expect them to just move on with life as if nothing happened.

So where do those who are hurting in ways other than the physical go for healing? There are multiple verses in the book of Proverbs telling us to seek council or wisdom. God is telling us we need to seek out those who can give insight, possibly from experience or training, concerning whatever the issue is with which we may need guidance. It is so much easier to make a good decision or choice if we have researched our options.

May any and all words of this book be taken in the right context and understanding. My sincere desire here is to inform, encourage, and lift up those who are dealing with difficult situations or circumstances in life. It is no secret that trials in life have the ability to discourage, or even ruin a relationship with God and man. Life is about choices, relationships, and maturing; May we all come to the point of making a positive decision to encourage each other unconditionally. May we also be humble enough to allow others to come beside us when they are needed, simply because together there is not only encouragement, but strength.

It certainly would be nice if there were a list of steps we could go through that would bring guaranteed relief in a timely manner if followed correctly. God is the only guarantee we have, and his word is the guide. It's imperative we comprehend, acknowledge, and gain the understanding that every person is unique, and that the difficulties of life do not work in a cookie-cutter manner with emotional beings. Even children in the same family, living in the same environment, will react differently to their surroundings.

When you or someone you know is dealing with one of life's hurts, trials, or an undesired circumstance, we tend to automatically assume that whoever is involved, must have done something to bring the present situation upon himself. That is possible but not always the case. Please don't judge or jump to a conclusion without knowing all the details or facts.

It is not our place to judge but to love unconditionally. Somebody may have done everything right and still can be a victim of circumstance. To back that claim up, I reference 2 Samuel, chapter 11, where Uriah, Bathsheba's husband, was killed because of David's sin.

Uriah was a soldier under King David. When David's lust got Bathsheba, Uriah's wife, pregnant, he tried to cover up his sin by calling her husband home, hoping he would spend time with his wife and think the baby was his. However Uriah did not do as David had hoped, so out of desperation the King sent his devoted soldier into the heat of the battle, knowing exactly what would happen. David committed murder to cover up his adultery, at the expense of an innocent man.

Solomon also informs us in Ecclesiastes 9:11, "The race is not to the swift or the battle to the strong, nor does food come to the wise, wealth to the brilliant, or favor to the learned: But time and chance happen to them all."

Life itself teaches us that the results desired are not always what come to be. One might even say to expect the unexpected. None of us have a get-out-of-trouble-free pass regardless of who we are, as told to us in Matthew 5:45. "He causes his sun to rise on the evil and the good, and sends rain on the righteous and the unrighteous." This is referring to God himself, who is in control of all things.

Some readers may wish to express how God hates the bad or negative attitude, and by dwelling therein may be committing sin. Suffering or the emotions that go with it do not automatically equal sin. God gave us these emotions, and he tells us in Ecclesiastes chapter three there is a time for all of them. Just because someone is dealing with difficult issues or a storm in life, and may express the negative things that accompany it, does not mean they have the wrong attitude or are committing sin. They most likely are trying to sum up what has happened, how it changes their life, and what direction to take next. We live in a world where things do go wrong, and we need to acknowledge the bad before we can put it into proper perspective.

This book will bring out some negative circumstances so that we can explore and understand how they influence us.

Only when we gain understanding can we make informed decisions for the positive results we desire. I don't believe God wants us to hide our heads in the sand of ignorance. I'm sure you did not sign up or volunteer for whatever the issue is with which you are dealing. God is not a God of confusion, but a God of peace, and if you are reading this book, it's probably because you desire that peace.

Many comforts, relationships, or abilities we have, giving personal satisfaction and enjoyment during our time on this earth, may be taken away without warning. Relationships can change or be strained through death, distance, or some other circumstance. Even our physical abilities may change due to age or some unforeseen incident. Your life may have hit a brick wall and come to an abrupt halt, stuck for the moment in uncertainty; you may be frustrated as you try to make decisions with inadequate information or experience.

However, hope cannot be taken away. Hope is belief in something or someone. Never convince yourself or believe there is no hope. Don't ever quit or give up trying. Hope is what gives us stamina, drive, and a reason to press on. Hope means there is always a chance or possibility for something or someone to change. As long as you are alive, there is hope!

What Is Hurt?

It is imperative to explore the meaning or have an explanation of what hurt is, thus helping us understand when we are actually dealing with it. The logical place to go for this revelation is a dictionary, which hopefully gives us a broader understanding of clarity and meaning.

The dictionary definition of *hurt* is *a negative effect*. It can be in the form of pain, setbacks, or some other sort of difficulty causing us to experience something undesirable or unpleasant.

My personal definition of *hurt,* is when we are plunged into a chaotic, uncontrollable, undesired circumstance. It can include pain—both physical and emotional—loneliness, uncertainty, inadequacy, inability, and even misunderstanding.

The degree of suffering a hurt, or how much impact it has on us, can be as broad as the world is big. The severity of an unpleasant circumstance seems to amplify with time. The longer it drags on, the more severe it becomes in our minds. If it doesn't last very long, we find it tolerable and easier to forget about or deal with. However, if it continues for a period of extended time or comes with more pain and sorrow, our natural human nature tends to embrace a negative attitude.

We as humans have a bent toward dwelling more on the negative things that surround us than on the positive. This is really a backward or wrong approach to changing our outlook. Good or positive things are always there, even in our darkest times. We tend to overlook them, believing they have somehow lost their value in comparison to whatever storm in life is currently overwhelming us.

Everybody can come up with a few examples of how he has been hurt or had to deal with trials at some time during his life and the results of how it has influenced or changed him, good or bad. Yes, there are scars, but those are to remind us later what we've been through, lest we forget the decisions and change of priorities we may have made during those detours.

Now that we've got a general grasp of what hurt is, let's take an in depth look at each of the four categories mentioned earlier. By doing so, we can see not only how they differ, but also help us understand what role each has in our daily lives.

1. Physical: Physical hurt is generally associated with the human body and our strength or ability to function. Sometimes things come into our physical lives that cause us to be less functional. We are not all created with the same physical characteristics. We differ in sex, capabilities, and size. We are all made unique, and it's not only possible we are affected differently

by the same situation but probable. Some people are born with physical problems, and some have something happen in life that changes them in a manner, where they must deal with a bodily issue for the rest of their life. Our physical pain or trial, whether short or long term, can also have implications in other areas of who we are, by the way we choose to emotionally handle the disruption or change that has occurred.

2. Financial: Financial refers to our ability to buy, sell, or manage our resources in order to provide for our needs or wants. We have a certain amount of money or resources to work with, and we try to adjust our lifestyle and goals to work within those means. However, we all know only too well that things don't always go as planned. A financial hardship may come because of some physical injury or sickness, maybe an accident, divorce, gambling, death, your job, or the possibility-some bad decisions were made. The list of financial needs or hardships is endless.

3. Emotional: Emotions are feelings or opinions through reasoning, with whatever information we have accumulated. Emotions can be swayed or challenged by outside influences. Our emotions are directly influenced by what life has dealt us and certainly by those with whom we associate. Low self-esteem, broken relationships, and uncertainty, are heavy burdens that can directly affect our emotions. The most important point I wish to make about emotions is the attitude

that accompanies it. We all experience different emotions as life happens; however, we choose the attitude regardless of the emotion a situation brings, and that attitude's influence is greater than the emotion itself.

4. Spiritual: The spirit is the heart, soul, and mind. The connection to the religious or sacred things of life, our core beliefs, our inner being or will, non materialistic. The important challenge is to know who God, the ultimate supreme spiritual being is. Having a genuine relationship with him, allows us to stand strong during trying times. When things go awry, you probably question what truth is, what you really believe is truth, and if there are absolutes. The spiritual is the core of what you believe life is based on through faith and hope, the unseen principles of what allows things to exist and function.

Each one of these four areas can bring a hurt or difficulty so severe, it can dominate our entire being. As much as we don't want to admit it or even bring the discussion up, there are times of despair when we all may entertain thoughts of giving up or quitting because it's just too hard, or we convince ourselves it doesn't make any difference anyway. It is not wrong to evaluate your life. If we never took stock of whom we were or what our priorities are, we would eventually become a society of directionless robots.

The important factor during these times of personal evaluations, is not that we are thinking about them, but actually doing something to improve ourselves or circumstance with the right attitude and motivation, thus allowing God to use whatever our situation is for his glory.

During times of hurt or personal struggles, we make choices that are usually based on protecting ourselves, such as ending a relationship for physical or emotional reasons. We may become selfish with the money and resources we have, justifying it with the "me first, I've earned it" attitude. In the spiritual, we become easily frustrated when things we have prayed for or believed in have different results than we expected or hoped for.

The deeper one gets into something, the harder it is to get back out. The tendency in extreme cases is to avoid those who seem to have given up hope, lest we be somehow sucked into it and feel the pain, sorrow, or get hurt ourselves. Those are the times the hurting person needs someone to willingly come alongside, to share the burden in an unconditional, nonjudgmental manner, regardless of what choices they may have made previously or how they got there in the first place. What if you were the one who needed a shoulder to lean on? Would you desire someone to give a pity party affirming your bad luck with no real encouragement or direction, or wish for hope through burdens shared by one who is tender in spirit?

Personally I was helped the most by those who had no personal agenda to fulfill, but gave of their time along with straight and blunt answers when I requested their input.

Life's detours, interruptions, and difficulties that cause hurt, pain, and disappointment are too numerous to name. Obviously I can't name everything (I'd probably miss your particular misfortune if I tried), but I think we can agree all hurts and circumstances are not the same. They come in varying degrees of difficulty and timelines. Sometimes we may even experience more than one type of hurt or hardship at the same time—and usually do. For instance, someone is sick, and the hospital bills add up, leaving them with not only physical pain, but financial stress as well.

We may not be able to control the physical or financial, but I strongly believe we make choices when it comes to the emotional and spiritual, choices to have the right attitude, seek and acknowledge God, give him our burdens and submit to his will. Yes, there are some emotional diseases that need medical help, but most of us can't use that excuse.

One thing is for sure. Nobody is exempt from feeling some kind of *hurt* during his or her lifetime, both directly and indirectly. We live in a sinful world full of uncertainty, disillusions, pain, sorrow, and death. Hurt can come in the form of one thing or many. It can vary in degrees of difficulty and may be of short endurance or a lifetime of challenges. Whatever or whenever things come that challenge and disrupt our comfortable world, we need to look at them as opportunities to grow in maturity, while accepting the changes with the right attitude.

My Story

Back to the phrase mentioned in the first chapter: "everybody has a story to tell." Although that is a true statement, no story is really complete until the end of life. Our lives are full of little stories that together make up our entire story. Even after your life has ended in death, the story continues with each person you have touched during your time on this earth.

What kind of legacy do you wish to leave? What will those who know you now say about you? Are you content with their answer to that question? I sincerely hope not, because God uses words like: seek, go, and persevere, never telling us we have arrived or have the right to quit. So your story, regardless of where you are now, is only partially complete. All of us, for as long as we live, are in a continuous process of becoming who we are.

Hopefully I can help you see beyond yourself through my experience to understand how we all need support in life at some time. As I have experienced over the past few months, I can wholeheartedly confirm that when others come alongside in difficult times, it creates a bond beyond understanding.

All right, I know you are probably asking what my trial is and how God brought me to this point in my life. I wish to tell my story to encourage and inform those suffering through some difficulty, they need not bear it alone. The reasons for writing down these thoughts are not only to help those hurting, but especially to inform those who desire to help, understand the feelings, thoughts, motivations, and how God may want them to fit into the picture.

I realize my particular type of endurance or trial may not be the same as yours, but I sincerely believe we all deal with the same types of questions and the emotions that parallel them.

God got my attention by showing me he was in control and not me. He used the economic downturn as his tool to turn life upside down, not only for me, but also my wife of thirty plus years.

We had enjoyed approximately twenty years of good living while I worked in the tool-and-die trade before I decided to venture out on my own.

I was self-employed in the metal working industry for eleven years before my world fell out from under me. Other than some farming experiences while growing up, tool-and-die was the only industry I had ever worked in.

Trying to build a future the American way, I had invested in industrial machinery and commercial real estate. We had even mortgaged our house to build the business when the market was in its boom.

Along with the major population in America, I believed that with hard work, dedication, and self-discipline, long-term financial goals could be achieved. With the rapid devaluation of most of these items over a period of only about a year, I was soon upside down in my debt-to-value ratio, as many others can relate to.

It didn't take many months before the bank thought of me as a high risk; they stepped in, forcing me to permanently close the doors of my business and lay off my four remaining employees. An auction followed where supply, demand, and depreciation gave me nickels on the dollar.

At the same time, manufacturing jobs disappeared at an alarming rate in the United States, especially in Michigan, where we were located. Many other metal working shops in the area closed about the same time, adding scores of workers seeking employment. The only industry I really ever knew, in a sense, had come to a screeching halt. Now there were only a fraction of the jobs that had existed just a few years ago, with most tooling work either going overseas, or slowing to a trickle because of the economy lacking demand.

As an owner, I was able to collect unemployment for only a couple of months. With jobs at a premium, I found myself in the position of being slightly older than most places desired to hire. Although I am a state certified toolmaker, I did not have any other degree behind my name, which is required in most job markets today. I was only able to bring in minimal income by working part time and temporary jobs.

In less than two years, my wife and I had lost everything materialistic that we had worked for over the past thirty years. I did not have a full-time job, and unemployment was no longer available to me. Additional stress came on me personally because my wife had been a stay-at-home mom and depended on me for her financial needs. I felt I had let her down.

We changed our lifestyle to adjust to the lack of income. We had no steady income or health insurance for over a full year. We sold all our liquid assets and opted for vehicles of lesser value.

It is very hard to give up the things we enjoy spending our time on and a life we are used to, not only due to the social class and the fulfillment they give, but also the humility that comes with it. Maybe life was just too full of time consuming personal passions, so God decided to relieve us of some worldly possessions, leaving room for his blessings.

Like many others, I had my hands so full God couldn't hold them or fill them. God wants us to hunger and thirst after him, not after the material things of this disappointing world. The things we see are temporal, and the things not seen are eternal. When disappointment or negative circumstances come into our lives, we make choices of priority and attitude. I encourage you to seek God and his will, not blame him and lose an opportunity to grow or be used by him.

When things looked bleak for my wife and me, one of the major efforts I made was to pray for wisdom. My concept of what wisdom was, is to have enough common sense to make good choices. Only after enduring many days and months of disappointment and despair did I grasp what wisdom really is.

The definition of *wisdom* in the dictionary is *the knowledge and experience needed to make sensible decisions.* It was the *and experience* phrase that I had not anticipated. The conclusion I soon drew was that some of the things I was enduring were a direct answer to my ignorant prayer. I was gaining the wisdom I prayed for through what I was experiencing. You see, my prayers were answered, but not the way I had anticipated; however, I do feel blessed because of it. Now I feel I have gained some understanding as well as having grown in wisdom.

There are multiple other hurts my wife and I have experienced during this time of reevaluating life; however, I hope I have told enough of what we have endured to convince those reading that this is not just a made-up story so I have a reason to write a book. I really can relate to the emotional roller coaster of uncertainty and the disappointments that life brings. I also have had to make choices I thought I never would, and have learned to live by faith and depend on God. I know first hand what it feels like to be the recipient of other people's generosity and the humility that comes with it.

You may be wondering how long the situation of financial decay I am personally dealing with has lasted, and if I have recovered. The end I hope is getting nearer, but has not yet been revealed. At this time it has been two full years of uncertainty. Many changes have taken place and many difficult choices had to be made. I am once again working full time in the metal working industry, as an employee of a former competitor.

Well, that's my story so far; I'm not dead yet. Maybe you can relate to my story and are asking questions like, *so now what? Is God really there and listening to our prayers?* I assure you, he is. I truly believe Romans 8:28: "And we *know* that in all things, God works for the good of those who love him, who have been called according to his purpose."

Don't misinterpret what is being said here. "Work together for good" does not necessarily mean our good, but for his purpose and glory. We need to let God use us unconditionally in the same way he loves us. I'm excited to share some thoughts, experiences, and spiritual lessons I have learned and continue to learn. To encourage those who wonder if they will ever experience passion for anything again.

I do believe in hope, because hope is of the Lord. Most people who know me say I'm an optimist, always expecting the best. That's probably true, but only because I believe God's word is true, and I choose to live by faith with hope. Just knowing God cares for me inspires me to never quit or give up on hope.

It's comforting to find a passage in God's Word that helps fill the need of encouragement, or the desired peace for the difficulty we are presently experiencing in life.

One particular passage I have gone to has been Psalms chapters thirty-three and thirty-four. It reminds me to praise God because of who he is. I am encouraged when I read in his word that he knows and cares about me. It tells me God has not abandoned me, a great comfort during trying times! It also states what my responsibilities and privileges are in my relationship with God.

God uses average, ordinary people for his glory if they have a right and willing heart. Sometimes we feel God is out there somewhere but not listening to our pleas for help. In Hebrews 13:5, he reminds us, "Be content with what you have, because God has said, never will I leave you, never will I forsake you."

God never leaves us, but we sometimes go off on our own for whatever reason. Just like relationships with other people, we need to spend time with God to have a relationship, a true connection. We do this by reading his word and spending time alone in prayer with him.

Little prayer, little power; some prayer, some power; much prayer, much power. James 5:16: "The prayer of a righteous man is powerful and effective." Communication with God is vital, but we must ask in God's will and not for selfish gain. James 4:3: "When you ask you do not receive, because you ask with the wrong motives, that you may spend what you get on your own pleasures."

Prayer is the most important tool any believer has. I am disappointed when I hear a believer say, "The least I can do is pray." Don't you realize that prayer is not the least, but the most? That should be where we go first; it's direct access to the creator of the universe with unlimited resources, the ultimate power who has the ability to help. Prayer is a tool that can be used on behalf of yourself or others, and I strongly urge you to pray for each other first, whether you are the hurting or the helper.

I know my time with God has dramatically increased. I am very thankful for the disappointing things in life that have driven me toward a deeper relationship with my creator. He does take care of his own; he knows you better than you can imagine. Read Psalms chapter one hundred and thirty nine; it will give you a glimpse of who God is.

Connections

It is almost impossible to live on this earth alone as the population grows and secluded areas disappear. We find our existence interconnected in multiple ways. Our supply lines to food, shelter, transportation, utilities, or any other daily requirements, hinge on the services and abilities of others we may not even know. This world of existence is about relationships, dependence, and doing our part.

Although we depend on each other for so much, things don't always work in the flawless manner we expect. Our resources or abilities change, accidents happen, personalities collide. When they do, someone suffers the consequences.

If you are the one hurting, typically one of the first types of questions or comments you express will be; *Where is God now? Why does he not answer my prayers? He seems to have abandoned me. I just don't feel his presence.* Relax; you are normal when you ask these questions. You might question everything from your own responsibility, to how God fits into the present situation. If we did not have difficulties in our lives, would we become complacent, routine, or stuck in the rut of self-sufficiency?

A critical point in the process of dealing with hurt is for the hurting person to let others in. I know we have our pride and dignity. We certainly don't want others to know we may be weak or perish the thought, that we just can't solve the problem on our own. We deceive ourselves when we think we can handle it alone, causing us to miss out on the benefits of having someone walk beside us.

The common phrase "out of sight, out of mind" is one many of us embrace and practice simply because we do not know what to do. Rather than offend someone, we avoid them. In our own mind, we believe we have done them a favor, but the reality is we have done just the opposite by making them believe they are unimportant and not worth our efforts.

Having the willingness of caring people, choosing to be available and willing to walk beside the hurting, is what completes and connects us as humans.

Life is usually a series of steps when it comes to the unexpected interruptions in our structured routines. Initially, when things get off the beaten path, we are self-confident and are usually able to fix things ourselves.

The next time, it is slightly more complex or difficult, so we ask someone to come alongside for both moral support and their ability or resources.

Then it may get even harder, but we somehow are still able to make adjustments, possibly even a drastic one, to find a suitable solution while maintaining control.

Finally the circumstance has deteriorated so far that it becomes obvious even to ourselves, that we are no longer in control. We can only cry out to God the ultimate power for help in our uncontrollable, humanly impossible-to-overcome situation of pain and hurt. Getting to the point of understanding our delicate position of dependence on God, can come quickly or take a lifetime, and sadly for some, never.

I suggest we need a little push from the difficulties in life, forcing us not only to pursue God, but to reap the reward of a deeper relationship with him. We can and do become lazy, especially when it comes to acknowledging God in every aspect of our lives. As difficult as it is for most of us to admit, there are times in life we get a little too comfortable where we are. We need a push from some outside circumstance to force us to mature, or be stretched outside of our comfort zone.

Sometimes we build relationships through unexpected means. Not necessarily of choice but of need. The bond this type of relationship holds, is rooted in understanding through experience.

Let me ask a pointed question. Do you personally know God and does He know you? We really can't expect God to help us if we don't have a relationship with him, can we? Would you be willing to help a complete stranger? It's definitely easier to help a friend, and we are usually willing to help a close family member even quicker. Helping or being helped by those we have a relationship with is the point. Common sense tells us that those we have close connections with, those we care about, are the ones we willingly give of ourselves for. God did that for all of mankind and desires we have a relationship with him.

Having a relationship with God means admitting to him you are a sinner (an imperfect person) and asking for his forgiveness, acknowledging and believing that Jesus Christ died on the cross and rose from the grave for you, trusting Jesus to be your savior for all of eternity. Then, like any other relationship you value, spend time with God in prayer and his word.

Relationships take time! I'm not referring to the aspect of time in years but the time we spend daily. What if God gave you as much attention as you give him? Each one of us desires time with those we feel close to, like our spouse, family member, or a friend. Those are the people who enrich our lives and give us a sense of belonging.

God is always there; we are the ones who choose to spend the time with him. We should want to have constant communication and a growing relationship with him, like a parent, brother, sister, or close friend. Then when times of trouble come, you may rest in the assurance that he knows who you are and desires to bring you through it as a child he loves and cares for. Notice I did say *through*, not *into*. He wants us to complete or finish life with the goal of spiritual maturity. The hard part for us is allowing God to be in control while going through the trials, difficulties, hardships, and hurts. Ultimately these things challenge us to grow into a mature believer for his purpose and glory, but when we are struggling through them, time drags, and we want relief.

Sometimes an issue we are dealing with cannot be immediately resolved due to the timing, like a seed planted in late fall will not grow until the environment is right in the springtime. When we do not see immediate results or solutions to the present situation, our lack of a patience attitude wants to give up hope. We willingly accept it when a doctor tells us the broken leg will take eight weeks to completely heal, but when it comes to non-physical areas of life we expect immediate results. We need to choose the right attitude regardless of the difficulty, along with the understanding that it's not all about what we think should happen or when.

Self is usually our biggest enemy. We think we have all the answers along with the ability or resources to make it on our own. We take pride in being self-sufficient and certainly don't want to express any weakness or venerability by admitting we might fail. Usually our first mistake, because of pride, is not allowing anybody to get close enough to give the needed input or help during times of personal weakness. We continue to walk aimlessly and hope for the best, thinking it can't be that bad, still convincing ourselves that we can handle it alone.

Men probably deal with this factor more than women, due to the fact that men have more of a tendency to think they are independent, self-sufficient, and invincible. Peer pressure sometimes pushes men to succeed no matter what, through constant competition. Men are not out to play the game, they are out to win. Failure makes them susceptible to the ridicule of other men and is a major blow to their ego.

Generally speaking, men have very few close friends. They hardly ever open up with emotions or intimate feelings that might expose them as weak and not in control. The world's view of what a man is or should be, does not allow for weakness or vulnerability. Men generally don't seek council, because to be a real man they must work it out on their own (maybe that's why they don't like to ask for directions!). All decisions and actions come from whatever bits of information and other knowledge they have acquired in the past. Men like to base decisions on logic or what they see as practical, usually pushing emotions into the background.

Women generally have many friends, so are likely to receive greater input this way. They also have a tendency to base their decisions on emotion over logic. They are quick to share things of the personal nature with other women, finding emotional support and strength to endure the hardship. They seem to be better communicators than males when it comes to difficulties in life.

These observations are not always the case, as there are always exceptions. Because we all fit in the male or female category, this information is nothing new to anybody. I'm simply giving a generalization to stimulate your thinking as to how we differ in our approach to life. We need to take as much information into account as possible to have a better understanding of how decisions are made. Having a better understanding of how everything involved influences us or the other person, allows opportunity to make informed, wise, and helpful decisions the first time instead of by trial and error, as is usually the case. That type of instinctive behavior, usually adds to the frustration our present difficulty has already produced.

Sometimes we avoid people because we want to be left alone, possibly for a good reason, like being stressed out. We certainly don't want to offend someone during our time of irrational, although legitimate thinking. That's a logical thought pattern, but in doing so, we may have cheated ourselves out of having a friend come alongside for support.

There are times when we try hiding from everything and/or everybody. I'm not trying to justify this behavior, just acknowledging that it happens. However, in reality, we are actually saying, *I can't and I won't deal with this, I don't need others, I want to wallow in my self pity, and I can handle this alone.* The blunt truth is; this behavior is not only selfish but is also a lonely path to personal destruction.

This is not the attitude God had in mind when he created us as relational beings. We need someone to come beside us to buffer or absorb, giving us support and encouragement when we face difficult situations. With the needed help, we can actually say, *I can and I will.* That help comes best from those who have experienced a similar disruption in life.

Hurt, regardless of what type it is, affects more than just the one individual involved. The best example to portray this affect is marriage. When two people live shared lives, there really is no separation when it comes to the hurt of one of them. The other has no choice but to be drawn into the hurt or difficulty, maybe in a different manner, but they are still influenced by the circumstance. Their life will also be altered to accommodate changes, simply because they are married and share time, space, and resources. Sometimes the hurt can involve both of them equally.

When a hurt includes a married couple, they probably have different viewpoints of how to handle it, because males and females think differently as previously stated. Although easier said than done, each needs to try understanding how the other is thinking, feeling, and desiring to deal with the difficult situation. The outcome has a bearing on them both and not necessarily in the same way. Communication is the key. People are not mind readers, so talk to each other! Remember, marriage takes two; you are not the only one involved. God gave you a mate to help share responsibility and burdens.

Other ways a hurt can directly affect you is because of family. It could even be someone outside the family that you depend on or with whom you have a personal relationship. Family includes the people you are connected to for life, those you care about because of shared time and space. A strong, caring family gives each of the members the ability to feel the agony or joy another may experience due to the emotional connection and the direct involvement of shared lives.

We are all connected to someone somewhere and for good reasons: strength, support, encouragement, and the assistance needed when one's personal ability is lacking.

How the Hurting Feel

People are curious and are quickly drawn to the troubles of others. That's why the nightly news and some reality shows are major parts of all the television networks. It's usually someone's demise or heartless acts toward others that have the biggest crowd of observers. We are all curious about some new development from the normal routines, especially in the lives of those we know, and we usually have an opinion as to how it should be handled.

Although we are compelled to find entertainment in the miseries of others, compassion is another human trait God installed in us. We usually root for the underdog and wish for the right thing to be done with the best possible outcome.

Trials, hurt, and unplanned or undesirable situations that disrupt our *normal* lives can come at any time. We never grow out of the possibility or become exempt with age, status, wealth, or even maturity

In the beginning of a difficult situation, friends and relatives are willing to give advice and are right beside you.

However, after time, when things don't seem to be working out or changing for the better, they have a tendency to back off, possibly thinking they can't really help, or feeling they may make the situation worse and be blamed for it. They may also get tired of it, because they have lives of their own to live. They begin to reason it's not really their problem.

For those who genuinely care enough to come alongside, let me tell you how the hurting person feels.

Below are seventeen descriptive words with a short explanation as to how or what the hurting will be or already are experiencing. The list, I'm sure, doesn't hit everything, but what is here can show the hurting person that they are experiencing normal emotions and reactions, and the helper/supporter can see by the list, what their friend or family member is dealing with.

These descriptive words do not fit every situation or type of hurt. They can also come at different times during the healing process and sometimes long after. When a particular hurt in life seems to have passed, we soon forget that those who have endured it, must now live with the scars and the life changes it brought.

Please read these with an open mind. Think on them; don't try to justify or blow them off as if they mean nothing. Let the words and their explanations penetrate your thinking, maybe even have someone in mind as you read the list. If nothing else, think of your own life and how these descriptive words of emotion have influenced the difficulties you have experienced and how you may have dealt with them.

- Exposed—Placed on a pedestal for all to observe instead of hidden in the normal routines of life. They think and feel they are on public display and that everybody is talking about them.

- Vulnerable—They feel weak, believing others will take advantage of them in their weakened condition.

- Fearful—Experiencing the unknown is scary; it's intimidating to deal with things someone is not accustomed to. One particular fear is making wrong decisions that could result in losing ground.

- Inadequate—Inexperience in a particular circumstance. They are asking, *How can I do this? I can't handle what is happening. I'm not smart enough, strong enough, or I lack the necessary abilities and resources.*

- Robbed—Time and control has been taken from them. They are at the mercy of others, who make decisions for them. They are unproductive and set aside for as long as this issue dominates their life.

- Humiliated–Their reputation is tarnished or ruined; their place in society has changed. They feel they have lost the respect and favor of others. Whatever dignity they had possessed, is lessened or eliminated.

- Valueless—To society and family, simply because they are no longer involved or complete. They feel unproductive and pushed aside. Self worth is all but gone.

- Selfish—The spotlight is on them because things are not the norm. They have lost control and feel guilty for being the center of attention.

- Despair—Life's plans and goals have been changed without their consent or input. Hopes and dreams have been put on hold, or from their viewpoint, completely dashed. There is nothing to look forward to.

- Tired—Struggles in life wear people out. It's harder to keep up when dealing with additional issues in life. It can be even more tiring with time and severity.

- Judged—They self judge, feeling they must have done something to deserve what they are enduring. They also feel those who know them are forming opinions as to why they are going through this.

- Frustrated—This is not the way they wanted it or planned it, and they can't seem to fix it. Whatever they have tried or are trying does not bring the desired conclusion or change.

- Confused—Not sure what they should be doing or what the solution is, they are lost for direction. They are overwhelmed as they try to deal with many new and unknown things.

- Stagnant—Life is stuck, and they can't seem to get it moving. They feel left behind and wish for life to get back to a normal routine of usefulness.

- Stressed—Trying to accomplish or deal with things beyond the norm adds strain to life, usually due to lack of time or resources. Too many things to deal with at the same time overwhelms and frustrates.

- Dependent—The option to be independent and self-sufficient has been ripped away. They know they need help but hate the intimidation that come with it. They feel like a burden on family and friends. It's possible they may become recluse and withdrawn, trying desperately to hold their own.

- Lonely—Others withdraw to give them space, or don't want to adjust their own routines to fit the now changed lifestyle of the hurting. They feel set aside from the usual communication, activities, and friendships.

- Alone—They wonder if anyone else really relates to the difficulty they are facing. Change of lifestyle and emotional stress disrupts relationships.

They want to give up because they are just worn out, tired, confused, and uncertain what the future holds for them. They feel condemned, judged, second-class, and sometimes even get the feeling of only being tolerated by those who once seemed to care. Things will never be the way they were; personal lifestyle changes are forced upon them without their consent.

The new normal will take time to make necessary adjustments. Changes can be difficult to accept or implement. The lifestyle and comfort zone once enjoyed are suddenly and abruptly altered, forcing them to make adjustments they didn't necessarily want and certainly didn't think they would ever need to make.

If they could escape from the present predicament, go back in time, or hide from all the negative issues bombarding them, most normal people would not hesitate to take one of those options. However, those options are usually not available, so we grudgingly face what we must.

If someone is willing to come alongside, the burden shared is easier to bear. We all need encouragement sometime during life. Encouragement can be as simple as knowing someone cares. A listening ear, a smile, a hug, or even time spent—these things don't really cost the giver much.

One of the unspoken fears the hurting deal with is how others view them now. It's probable with whatever life has dealt you that your status has changed. It may be a divorce, a child, some other relationship, the death of someone close, even a job change, any of which can immediately alter your social status. Another hurt with dramatic results can be a financial decay, which can quickly ostracize you from the lifestyle and friends that you had been involved with and enjoyed. There could be an accident, sickness, or disease, causing limitations on your body and abilities.

It is not necessarily that those around or involved in our lives ceased to care. So please don't make a quick decision to judge them, as you wish them not to judge you.

A few things happen during these transitions we need to observe. If someone has never endured the difficulty you have, it is next to impossible for them to totally understand. They may hold back, fearful of the situation; just like you, they also fear the unknown of how to react to your circumstance. Next, the hurting individual needs to understand it is their life that is changing, not someone else's. This is hard to swallow, as we are quick to compare and rationalize the picture from where we are. We may even secretly wish our difficulty on someone else because we feel they deserve it more than we do. It is only a normal human reaction, to process in our minds all the reasons we don't deserve what has transpired.

Let me be frank: although this is hard to address, I feel it really needs to be stated. When a person's life gets to the point of despair, when they see nothing left for them to look forward to except misery, suicide will cross their mind. It happens; we can't just sweep it under the rug or ignore it. It happens. I didn't say they considered it; I said it crossed their mind. It's because they are thinking of all the possibilities to change their present situation. We make choices every day, and it is the choices we make that define who we are. Hopefully, when someone thinks of the extreme choice of suicide, they quickly dismiss it and choose life, realizing there is hope, along with help, and love that can pull them through their time of bleak despair.

My comment to those considering taking their own life for whatever reason, is that you are valuable! Although you may not always see or feel it, others do care about you. What you do with your life has a direct impact on those closest to you. Please don't give up, choose life for them if not for yourself.

We do not get to choose what type or the degree of difficulty a trial in life brings us. But when such disruptions happen, we usually ask the "why me?" question. We will discuss that issue in the next chapter.

It does not take many years of living in this uncertain world, to draw the conclusion that it is much easier to look back to understand why things worked the way they did in our lives. Fortunately, we cannot see ahead; if we saw how much difficulty we could possibly be destined for, it might drive us to the grave prematurely. Having the present to deal with is probably pushing our limits already. God is merciful by allowing portions (and hopefully some relief between times of trouble) instead of all our trials at once.

First Corinthians 10:13 states: "No temptation has seized you except what is common to man. God is faithful, he will not let you be tempted beyond what you can bear. But when you are tempted, he will also provide a way out so that you can stand up under it."

It's not unusual to interpret temptation to mean our trials or difficulties. Just reading or hearing that verse makes most hurting people want to scream! They feel they have personally had to endure more than they can handle. They want relief or an answer now; the pressure is too great. They feel that all viable options have faded away and greatly desire to hide from life until things turn around.

Actually, this is a verse of encouragement! It reminds us we are not the first person who has ever endured a difficult challenge in life, and that God is there for us if we allow him to be. We can and will get through whatever our disruption is, with his help. Psalms 33:4: "For the word of the Lord is right and true, he is faithful in all he does." In a world full of trouble and uncertainty, there is comfort knowing that he is faithful. We can actually count on things being exactly like his word says, unlike the every-man-for-himself world we presently call home.

Another factor that plays a huge role in a hurting situation, causing much anguish and discomfort, is guilt. Guilt is a feeling of personal responsibility, blame, or accountability for how something has turned out. It is hard to portray in words how guilt influences our decisions. The guilt factor can be on both sides, from the hurting to the helper, and for different reasons. The hurting feels guilt for receiving undeserved attention and gifts. The helper may feel guilty for not being able to find the right words, not being able to be there at the appropriate time, or not having the necessary resources to give relief to someone in need. Both sides need to have the emotional flexibility and understanding to allow the other to be what they can, when they can. It simply boils down to: *Don't judge others and do the best you can with what you have.* We have a tendency to judge things we do not understand while shying away from things we feel we can't control.

Decisions to draw a conclusion as to why someone has a certain difficulty instead of loving them unconditionally, are made with the information we have, and more times than not we lack enough information to make a qualified decision, especially pertaining to other people's circumstance or situation. Is it that hard to give others the benefit of doubt, or to love them unconditionally as Christ loves us?

One critically important note I need to make to those whose friends or family are dealing with hurt or life changing-situations—if you are the person God wants you to be, the following four-word statement should penetrate deeply: You will also change. It's inevitable. Let me explain. Just by continuing the relationship you have with the hurting individual, you soon realize that your role as a participant has to change. The relationship cannot remain the same, simply because things are not the way they used to be. Therefore, you need to make adjustments in your own life to accommodate the changes in your friend's or relative's life.

If you desire to help yourself or others during trying times, you need to know how emotions and attitudes can and do play into relationships. Life is made up of personal choices and relationships. God made us to be relational, not lone rangers. We need each other, and we also need God, who just happens to be our ultimate source for everything.

Relationships take communication and consideration. The first thing required of you is the willingness to allow someone into your life at an intimate level. Helping or being helped is shared responsibility that can only happen if both sides trust each other and have the same goal. This principle is applicable not only for human interaction but also with God in our personal and spiritual lives.

Let me put it another way. It takes the right person at the right time, with the right attitude for the right purpose. Proverbs 17:17 says, "A friend loves at all times." We have all heard of fair-weather friends. When it benefits them, things flow smoothly, but when it might cost them more than they get, they conveniently become scarce. A friend loves at *all* times; love is a commitment. My dictionary tells me *commitment* is *responsibility*. Put yourself aside and take on the role of a true friend, regardless of your personal opinions. Remember, relationships take work or effort, including proper communication and consideration. Only when we grasp and embrace this reality can we properly share whatever the burden is.

Don't think of getting involved as a one-sided event. Yes, you may be the one doing all the receiving or all the giving at this present time; however as believers, we serve a God who rewards and gives blessings to those who do things with the right motivation and attitude. Consider the possibility of gaining a deeper relationship with others as well as growing in the knowledge and understanding of who you are as a child of the king. Don't do something out of duty or obligation, but with a willing spirit unto God.

So when something alters your lifestyle in a manner you do not prefer or did not plan for, where do you turn? Who do you go to for advice, support, or help? It is only practical we seek someone or something that has the ability to help us, a greater power than ourselves. For a child, it might be the parents, for an employee, a boss. If you got hurt physically, it only makes sense to see a doctor, or with spiritual issues to seek help from a spiritual leader. Even when your pets are in need of something, they come to you with anticipation of your being able to supply them with whatever they have need of.

Again, it is not wrong or degrading to seek help when we come to those times of uncertainty and direction changing phases during our lives. If we truly desire the support, insight, or assistance of someone who can be our strength, they can be found.

Why Me, Why Not?

Time to switch gears. So far, it seems everything has had some kind of negative overture. I do not wish to dwell on the negative, but I also do not wish to ignore what is part of the world in which we live. Let us take a look from a different perspective. Yes, there are positive things to talk about, even when it seems your world has turned upside down.

Did it ever occur to you that the situation God has allowed in your life is for the benefit of others? Maybe it's not even about you. Maybe God has given you the *responsibility* of being used for his purpose. We do not always see the whole picture or understand the whole issue; that's why Christ talked about living by faith so much. Don't think for even a split second that God doesn't know what is happening in your life.

Psalms 139:2–4: "You know when I sit down and when I rise. You perceive my thoughts from afar. You discern my going out and my lying down. You are familiar with all my ways. Before a word is on my tongue you know it completely, O Lord." Psalms 139:16: "All the days ordained for me were written in your book before one of them came to be." Matthew 10:30: "Even the very hairs of your head are all numbered."

Whatever has come into your life, God knows about it. He knows every little detail about you, right down to how and what you think. It is no mistake that *God has chosen you* for the circumstance you are now dealing with. We don't receive blessings without having a reason to receive them. Trials birth opportunity for us to make choices, and blessings are a direct result of making right choices. It is even possible you are blessed to be a blessing to someone else!

Somehow we perceive ourselves differently than those around us do. We think, *It can't happen to me, because I have lived right or have taken every possible precaution to prevent whatever from happening.* It doesn't always work that way. Nobody is exempt from having negative issues infiltrate their lives at some time. It will happen, and how we deal with it is what really matters!

In the prior chapters, we discussed what hurt is. Doing an about face, let's explore the opposite. Think about what life can be if no obstacles sidetracked you—how you want to live, what goals, ambitions, or things you desire to achieve. Who do you desire to become, or what could you possibly be remembered for?

Just changing our thought pattern to anticipated goals we feel can be accomplished, probably brought some kind of excitement, enthusiasm, and maybe even a smile to your face. If we are completely honest and had everybody take a survey, I believe the answers would be exactly the same. We all desire contentment, joy, peace, fair treatment, stability, friendship, and to be needed and loved while having our basic needs met.

Let me suggest a few things to broaden your thinking, possibly changing for the positive any perspective you presently embrace concerning what life may have tossed your way. This list is also a challenge and much needed information for the helper as well.

1. Let God use you. As hard as it is to be humbled into needing someone to come alongside in times of despair, allow God to supply through others with the mindset that all things come from him. You should thank him accordingly and ask him to bless those who have helped you (whether it be emotionally, financially, physically, or spiritually). Remember to keep any transactions of support as private and personal as possible, because God rewards those who do things in secret, and we certainly don't want others to lose their reward or blessing because we exploit their choice to help. I'm not saying don't thank the helper; I'm only suggesting you don't make it a public show. If you are the giver, sometimes being anonymous makes it easier for both sides.

2. Maybe God is using you as the needy person to allow someone else to be tested or used by God for his glory. Graciously let them help without trying to analyze why they are coming alongside. Whatever reason they have for supporting you is between them and

God. Your position of gratitude should not just be to the person of support but also to God, the ultimate provider. It is a privilege to serve God, and sometimes serving is being the one who needs help.

3. Encourage others. Being a needy person can and usually is very humiliating and sometimes intimidating, but we need to learn how to accept the position given us. Did it ever occur to you (as the needy person) that *you* can be the encourager and be blessed for it? Somebody is always watching you, trying to evaluate what type of relationship you have with God and man. Maybe they can see who God is by watching you under pressure. Consequently, they will either be encouraged or discouraged by the way you handle the trial. You may wish to disagree with that statement, but I believe you actually watch others when they endure hardships too, probably drawing some kind of conclusion as to how they let God fit into it. Maybe you are able to endure life's difficulty due to the faithfulness of a believer who set a good example for you. Let that be an inspiration for you to be faithful through your difficult circumstance.

4. Pray for others, taking the focus off self. God told us to love our neighbor. What can be a better way than to lift them up before the heavenly father? Just because you find yourself in an undesirable and uncomfortable environment does not make you the center of the universe. God is relational, meaning *we are not*

expected to endure or enjoy life alone, we belong together for the purpose of sharing and caring. As believers in Christ, we are family, brothers and sisters of equal value through the blood of Christ. Families should care about each other and live in unity. I encourage you to lift your family members up in prayer, in doing so you actually encourage yourself. When a prayer is answered, the family rejoices and is encouraged just by knowing God hears, answers, and is capable of doing the same for each of them. Praying for others shows genuine concern. We can pray anywhere, at anytime, and always have immediate, direct access to God the father through Jesus Christ.

5. It may not even be about you! God tells us he causes the sun to rise on the evil and the good. He sends rain on the righteous and the unrighteous. Sometimes you are just a victim of a sin-filled world. We don't always see the whole picture, so we must learn to live by faith, believing God knows best when he allows disruptive issues in our lives that may cause us to ask the "why" question.

6. Stop complaining for what God has allowed. We don't usually get a choice determining the type of trial that has infiltrated our lives, but we do get a choice in our attitude. Our attitude of acceptance or bitterness has a dramatic bearing on the outcome. Who are we trying to please? What do we want for an outcome? Do we place blame or find excuses for our behavior? Are we

looking for the opportunities the trial may allow that would not be there if things were "normal?" Will we miss out on blessings because of our attitude? James tells us in James 1:2 to "Consider it pure joy" when trials come. Most normal reactions to difficulties in life would rarely count as joy, but when we study in depth what results transpire from these undesired situations, it makes sense. Those who have gone through dark and treacherous times gain wisdom, understanding, and usually come out strengthened.

7. Some of life's detours may be considered training. Training is pushing one's self beyond normal routines. You may feel it's a school of hard knocks, but think of the change of pace as training to be a leader. Maybe the training is to help you relate to others who may soon be dealing with the same type of circumstance, thus building a relationship that certainly would not have been possible otherwise. Could it be this trial is to build your faith for some bigger responsibility God has destined you for in the future?

8. Strength comes from adversity; we learn much quicker from experience than any other way. All the things that are overwhelming you at the present time are nothing less than birth pains. We all know most women would rather not endure the pains before the birth of their children; however, without them, new life cannot happen. Is it possible the trial or situation

you are presently enduring is nothing less than "birth pains" for the new life God has for you?

9. You are being tested. That statement scares most people, but take a moment to think about the actual reason we are tested. Tests are usually for the purpose of revealing what you already know, and to bring out your ability to respond correctly. Don't fear a test, rather see it as a tool to better understand yourself. Whose responsibility? That's a penetrating question, especially when we are asking if we should come along side a hurting individual. When it's everybody's responsibility, somehow it becomes nobody's responsibility. We take it for granted, or maybe hope someone else will step up so we need not. My only comment regarding this pointed question is: Do for others what you wish they would do for you!

10. Change the *why* to *now what*? Look ahead and determine where this particular situation will take you. What possibility does this open for you that may not have been possible if it didn't exist? We all know it is very unusual for problems to just dissolve or work themselves out. We need to come to the undeniable conclusion that it does exist, we are involved, and for us to sit back and have a pity party benefits nobody. Think through the issue at hand and start making necessary changes to deal with what has transpired.

One of my favorite movies is the Christmas classic, *It's a Wonderful Life*. George Bailey, the main character, is stuck in a small town, always barely scraping by, taking responsibility without reward, for the benefit of others who are in need. The movie tells the story of how George had touched and influenced many people during his life, even though he felt like he only just existed. He watched friends and family excel, some in position, others in wealth. Meanwhile, he was stuck living in a rundown house, never able to find the time or resources, to leave the town he had come to regret. When his world fell apart due to someone taking advantage of him, he saw no reason to continue living and wanted to give up. He even went as far as to say he wished he had never existed.

Sound familiar? It shows how we compare ourselves to others, how we feel we fit in, or our desire to be treated in a fair manner. The picture applies to all aspects of our lives (physical, financial, emotional, and spiritual). We just want to give up or quit when things don't go the way we expect or desire. We have convinced ourselves that whatever effort we have put into something has not paid off, thus it was not worth our time or effort. To continue would only add personal disappointments. We get sick of giving without receiving; we expect to be rewarded for our time and to be treated fairly. When we feel slighted, our first instinct is to ask the selfish question, *What about me?*

There are two things I want to highlight here. The first is for you to think about how you affect others, what impact your life has on theirs. I'm not just talking physical; I want to emphasize the emotional and spiritual, as the two biggest and most important ways we connect to others.

Relationships matter. I cannot stress the importance of how we need relationships with other people. Relationships take communication from both parties. Please don't skim over this. Slow down enough to grasp the importance of that statement. Communication is an understanding with someone else.

One disclaimer I need to clarify: communication with someone does not constitute a relationship. A relationship takes commitment, understanding, and involvement!

Let your mind recall some of the ways you have been an impact on others, whether for the good or bad. Then think about how others have impacted you. Stop reading for just a few seconds and really think about how and why these people have influenced you.

Hopefully those who have impacted you, have done so for positive outcomes and growth in your life. If the impact was negative, it probably created some distance in the relationship. That's not the way God designed us to care for one another.

May whatever practical applications you have learned from your own life's experiences, cause you to influence others only in ways that may enhance their relationships with God and man. Positive things have a tendency to encourage; isn't that what we should be aiming for?

The second thing I want to inform you of: (Back to the movie *It's a Wonderful Life*) is the outcome of George's life. His world came crashing down, and he saw nothing positive to look forward to. He was then given the rare opportunity to see how the world may have been if he had not existed. He slowly began to grasp the reality of how he had helped others during their time of need. He saw how he had influenced a whole town for good. In his own time of need, they were there for him. The people loved him because of who he was. It was only then that he understood his purpose in life and gladly accepted it.

Although George was not well off financially, the people called him the richest man in town. It was because of the relationships he had with them, a connection by giving of self. Shouldn't that be the goal of all mankind? Can you imagine how the world might change for the better if we all lived with that philosophy?

My desire is to imbed something deep in your conscience, to remember you are not an island. An island is by itself with no connection. What good is it if we have a tongue and ears, but have nobody to share our thoughts with? We were made to walk through life together, to share the good as well as the issues less desirable. Life can and will unexpectedly change. When it does, remember that every person is valuable. We are all one-of-a-kind creations made by God himself. Don't ever think or let someone else persuade you that your life doesn't matter. It does!

When our comfortable world of routines and safety zones unexpectedly changes, we often find ourselves thrown into situations of confusion. It is common to experience intimating possibilities, not to mention the self-judging that so often accompanies such disorders. We hate the thought of having to depend on someone else for support. At these times in life, we feel vulnerable because of having to make decisions we never expected to make.

First Corinthians 14:33 says, "For God is not a God of disorder but of peace." Satan wants us to be confused, discouraged, and defeated. Don't let him have that pleasure. Seek God and the peace that only he can give; remember, he cares for every individual. That includes you!

God desires a relationship with each of us. He is committed, understanding, and wants to get involved. He is ready, willing, and able. As I stated previously, relationships take commitment and involvement on both sides. We humans are ultimately the ones who choose to complete the spiritual relationship by getting involved through prayer and the reading of God's word.

Sometime in life, we have no choice but to rely on the help of others. Treat others as you desire to be treated. Come gently alongside as a helper or humble yourself enough to let others in when you need them. It's tough on both sides; we don't want to get involved because it might cost us personally, or worse, it might affect who we are. We all know how to "Do the right thing" which is getting involved somehow. So what is it that gets in the way? I suggest pride and or selfishness.

Bankrupt is a nasty word that has weighed heavily on my mind due to what life had brought me personally. Maybe your situation isn't financial, but that doesn't mean you haven't experienced bankruptcy of another kind. A friend of mine who is suffering with a disease that limits his physical abilities told me he felt bankrupt. The term simply meant to him that the life he had known before the diagnoses, came to a screeching halt. He had no choice but to make drastic adjustments in his lifestyle, to accommodate what was taking place. He, like so many others, had come to a point of reevaluating life due to circumstances, learning to live life with a new set of rules.

Although it is hard to stop dwelling on what we may have lost, even when we know it was beyond our control, we really have very little choice but to go on by trying our best with what resources and abilities allow. Always remember how you influence or affect those around you! That should be the priority; that's what matters!

So again, why you? Let me ask you one more pointed question: who is better off in the end? It is the person who has been faced with circumstance that pushed them into growth. It's easy to be comfortable, and most of us would rather choose the easy way. When we lose things we took for granted or are forced to look beyond ourselves by needing others, we have the opportunity to grow, become thankful, and obtain a better understanding of why we exist. So why not you?

Mere Words

First impressions last. Have you ever noticed how quickly we categorize someone due to their speech? We judge them by the type of words they use and the tone of voice in which they express them. We may not even see the individual talking but quickly make a mental picture as to what type of person they probably are.

If the words and portrayal of them are the same type we use, there seems to be an instant bond because we feel they are somehow like us. If the words are soothing, comforting, positive, energetic, or interesting, we may desire to meet that person, with the possibly of getting to know them because of their charisma. If we are offended, put down, or challenged by someone's words, we tend to steer clear, not wanting them to influence us in like manner or allow ourselves to be brought to their level.

Can you see where I'm going with this? Our words can quickly make or break a relationship, and it's really hard to get a second chance. First impressions last, and it is very easy to ruin a reputation or lose respect. I need to caution you that it is not only the words themselves that matter but also how they are portrayed, presented, *and* perceived.

What is your motive when approaching someone? It shouldn't matter whether you are the one hurting or the one who is trying to help the hurting. Both sides need to realize that once something is said, especially in the wrong way, it can't be easily taken back. People are fickle; they don't forget, and second chances are hard to get. The very thing you desired to do, like encourage or find a common bond to build a relationship, instead may have discouraged both of the parties involved.

Sometimes our words, however innocently intended, can be devastating for those we wish to comfort. A young lady shared with me how when she lost her mother to cancer, those whose intentions were good made comments like: "*At least* she didn't suffer much," or "*at least* you still have your father." She told me those words cut deep because she felt in a sense they were not allowing her to grieve by trying to minimize the loss she felt.

The best insight I can give for a picture of in-depth understanding is to place yourself in the other person's shoes; try to see things from their point of view. This may help you relate and be sensitive not only to their situation, but their emotional and spiritual needs as well.

One aspect we tend to overlook on a personal basis is hearing ourselves speak. Our ears hear what comes out of our own mouths. We all know that if we hear something enough times, we start believing it. Sometimes things are said because we previously heard something similar somewhere and although we have not really thought it through ourselves or checked to see if it was solid information, we repeat it as if it were fact.

When a thought comes to mind and seems to fit, we express our opinion as if we have great insight. We have not only led whoever we are speaking to into believing that our words of advice are correct, but as we hear the words ourselves, we actually confirm in our mind our belief that what we have said is true. So not only are we possibly misleading others and abusing trust, but we may also be ignorantly misleading and deceiving ourselves. The message should be clear; make sure what you are saying is true and appropriate.

James 3:8 says, "But no man can tame the tongue, It is a restless evil, full of deadly poison." Words do matter; they do have affect on others for the positive or the negative. Those words spoken too freely have a lasting influence. I strongly urge you not only to be careful with your speech while trying to comfort or help someone, but to listen to what is coming from your mouth. Is it correct? Are you willing to take the heat if you misdirected a family member or friend? Is this the kind of encouragement you might appreciate if you were the hurting?

I too am convicted by these same questions, needing to give my thoughts and speech over to prayer daily. Certainly, the worst conclusion someone might draw at this point is to just give up and say, *I'm not willing to get involved if I might mislead or discourage.* That's nonsense and nothing less than an excuse. Take the option of getting involved, but be concerned that your words are fact instead of just giving your opinion and preferences. Yes, mistakes can and will be made, but we learn from our failures and grow. Trying is worth more than failure.

Don't ever believe your words will have no impact! Your words of encouragement, regardless of how little you believe they matter, are not wasted. A hurting person has the tendency to hold onto every word, and although they may not express it, really appreciate the effort you have made. They see beyond the words to the understanding, compassionate heart, behind what is being said.

Another issue of concern I have experienced due to the lack of income causing my own trial, are those who unwittingly (I do not hold that against them) tell me about all the good things going on in their lives: vacations, retirement, new toys, concerts, going out to eat, and even overtime at their jobs, just to let me know how good things are for them. I can only imagine as some read this, you're thinking, *So what? Why do you even bring these things up?*

When things are bad in your life, everything looks better than where you are. Troubles magnify the sting, of personal comforts that have been ripped away from you, including people and the comforts of a normal life.

All these positive issues for others, become hurtles of jealousy, envy, and desire, sometimes causing sin for the sufferer. They can be stark reminders of what has been removed, at least temporarily, from life. I am not trying to diminish the fact that life is good; as a matter of fact, I truly am happy and even pray things may continue to go well for others. What I am trying to say is that emotions are tender. Self worth is being questioned, and personal goals have been put on hold. Anything said, however intended, is perceived as a reminder of what life has become.

For the helper to make conversation with the hurting, showing genuine interest to be part of their life during difficult times is greatly appreciated. The hurting person sometimes has to deal with personal attitude issues the helper is not aware of. Although faultless of intentional conflict, when speaking of how good life is at the present time, it's possible to put the hurting person in a spiritual battle. Help them win the battle against the sins of envy, jealousy, and even bitterness. My only comment or point is to be aware of how the hurting person may place themselves in the conversation and what emotions it can bring up.

Words matter; I can say it no better or plainer than that. We can build up or tear down someone's self-esteem in just a few words. Once spoken, words cannot be taken back. We are given two ears to hear, and they are always open for business. However, we are given only one tongue with two guards: our teeth and lips. Maybe God gave us more ears than mouth because he wants us to listen more than we speak.

From my own experience and some observation of others dealing with negative circumstances in life, I want to make a pointed comment. If hurting people believe or feel that those around them, regardless of their intentions, are putting them on the defensive, they will avoid others simply for self-preservation.

If you notice someone withdrawing, don't give up. But have the right heart and motive as you continue being an encourager. That doesn't mean hound them, but rethink how you may have incorrectly approached and what might be a better way. An apology may even be necessary to gain back the needed respect, for you to be the vessel of encouragement.

A caring person considers the *how* and *what,* they are presenting with their words and attitude. Following are a few verses from the bible to illustrate this. Proverbs 17:22: "A cheerful heart is good medicine." Proverbs 10:32: "The lips of the righteous know what is fitting." Proverbs 15:1: "A gentle answer turns away wrath."

Words are usually direct from the heart; they are representations of our personal convictions and priorities. We can only be encouragers presenting the right words to those who need them when they need them, if we personally have the right relationships with both God and the one we are coming beside.

I cannot emphasis enough the importance of how our words *immediately* affect those around us. May we not only be aware of the words we speak, especially at the critical times of hurt during someone's life, but how we present them. Attitude, tone, timing, and compassion play major roles, and need to be properly spoken for your words of encouragement to be useful. If presented in a sarcastic, put down, badly timed, or a pull-yourself-up-by-the-bootstraps attitude, you will lose the opportunity to be of any help to the hurting person. They quickly write you off as someone who is only there to fill some kind of obligation or self-serving ego trip.

Common knowledge illustrates that some people have the ability to talk a lot and say nothing, while others speak very little but have much to say. One of my favorite sayings is *the more people talk, the less others listen.* We may laugh at that, but we all know it's true and probably can name a few people that either draw our respect, or disrespect because of this principle.

Speaking words is only part of the communication or connection we have with each other. When we speak, there are signs that are very visible to the other individual: the tone in which we present ourselves through body language, respect, and purpose. We read past the words to see if the person is genuinely concerned. These things may be in the form of eye contact, impatience, pity, interest, obligation, support, involvement, depth of conversation, time, and clarity.

Choose your words wisely and present them with a caring heart. Remember, the person you are trying to come alongside to help is hurting, and needs encouragement more than advice or opinions.

Words are like a pebble thrown into water. There may be a small splash when there is contact, but the ripple can go a long distance, influencing things far from the present situation.

Don'ts

There are times when we wish someone made a list of what to do or say, to bring about the right response in difficult situations. There are certain things we all do or say maybe even unwittingly, that simply irritate a situation instead of helping it. We usually don't realize we are going about it the wrong way, simply because we have not had a similar experience, and consequently do not understand how it effects the one we are trying to be sympathetic to.

Helping others to understand hurting people is my main goal in the next two chapters as I make a few suggestions from personal observation and experience. Those who are presently hurting will read this and find themselves relating to the different observations. As stated a few chapters earlier, sometimes we need help putting our feeling into words.

The following is a list of thought provoking observations that may be helpful in dealing with other people during times of hurt or difficulties. I have two categories, the Don'ts—what not to do or say, and in the next chapter, the Do's—practical ideas of how to come alongside someone when life has been altered without their consent.

Hurts usually come unexpectedly and without respect of who we think we are. The last thing anybody dealing with the negative aspects of life needs is for another human to kick them when they're down.

The only disclaimer I place before expressing the Don'ts, is that I know it is impossible to adhere to all of these. However, if we are aware of the things to avoid when trying to help others, we can be more effective in our efforts. The motto of a helper should be to encourage, not frustrate.

There will be times during your coming alongside someone that words will slip or conversations will slide into some gray areas. Don't let that discourage you as the helper. It means more to the hurting individual that you are trying, than the possibility of bringing negative results due to a few misplaced words. Effort trumps mistakes every time; the hurting person will overlook mistakes when they understand your heart. Be sensitive enough to say things in a considerate manner. First, the Don'ts:

1. Don't judge–
- You probably don't know the whole story.
- They may just be a victim of circumstance.
- Matthew 7:1–2 tells us we are judged in the same way we judge others. Do you want that pressure?

2. Don't give advice–
- Giving advice is like kicking them when they're down.

- In a sense, you are telling them you are smarter than they are, devaluing them.
- It's okay to give advice only if they ask for it.

3. Don't ask them "How are you doing?"–
- You may already know the answer, and for them to reply is bringing up negative feelings.
- Instead say, "It's nice to see you," or "I'm glad you're here. I'm happy I can be here with you."
- If they really want you to know something, they will tell you. Don't push it.

4. Don't forget them–
- Loneliness, boredom, and low self-esteem are enemies; they need companionship and support.
- Usually difficulties last for a period of time; they need you for as long as the trial exists.
- Even if the situation has run its course, there may be lasting effects.
- It's easier to avoid because you don't know what to do, but they need your presence.

5. Don't tell them about all the good stuff in your life–
- This may be exciting for you, but it simply reminds the hurting what life has dealt them.
- Examples: buying new things, vacations, retirement, job, bonus, children, or entertainment.

C.R. Boonstra

- Understand that they are trapped in an environment they can't escape. Don't dangle the carrot.

6. Don't join the pity party–
- They really need someone to encourage, not confirm how bad things are.
- Smile, listen intently, and allow them to express what they need to.
- Tell them you care and value them as a person.

7. Don't talk too much–
- Your presence is more valuable than any words you can muster.
- A thoughtless comment like, "It can't be that bad," won't win their trust or encourage them.
- Talking too much puts the attention on you, making them feel you are there for the wrong reasons.
- There are times when they don't want to talk. Nothing personal, just accept it.

8. Don't say, "Let me know what I can do for you."–
- The hurting person may not even know what you can do for them.
- They feel they are imposing on you by asking for anything and are not sure if you meant it.
- Just do something appropriate for the circumstance (gift card, meal, money, a night out to listen, mow the lawn, baby sit, clean their house, fix

78

their car, loan them something, go for a ride to-gether). Remember, it's difficult to accept things that can't be paid back. Give without obligation.

- Never make them feel they owe you; this adds fric-tion to the relationship and multiplies their pain.

9. Don't start sentences with
- "At least," "It could have been worse," "It will get better," or "You're not the only one."–
- In their mind, you are trying to minimize the issue, demoralizing them.
- In their present condition, nothing could be worse than what is or has happened.
- Allow them the necessary time to work through the emotions that we are created with.

10. Don't ask demanding questions, prying for more information; some things need to be kept personal.
- They already feel their life is a public display; allow them some privacy.
- Questions can frustrate, because of uncertainty. They may not have an answer.
- Let them know if they need a listening ear, you are available; then make yourself available.

11. Don't say you know how they feel.
- You do not truly understand unless you have been there; only then are you able to relate.

- Admit you do not know how they feel, but tell them instead that you feel for them.

12. Don't be the aggressor—

- Let the person you came to encourage lead or choose the conversation and topics.
- If you run the show, it sends a silent message that they are not important to you.

Although these things may sound discouraging to those wishing to come beside, I wish to point out that the feelings and emotions of the hurting are greatly influenced by your approach and especially your words. Starting off on the wrong foot will no doubt be very difficult to fix. The whole reason you came in the first place was to be of help. Therefore, come with the right mindset for them, as you would desire they might do for you if the tables were turned.

When hurt happens, in the mind of the one hurting everything is multiplied: the uncertainty, the self-worth, the doubts, and the perception of what others think. The same goes for the words you speak in a way that may come across negatively. Be careful and considerate; think how your words may be taken regardless of intent, before uttering whatever comes to mind just to make conversation.

Dos

I have not been fair with the don'ts if I leave you hanging with so many negatives. So what *can* you say or talk about? There is no cookie-cutter answer to that question, simply because different situations demand different solutions. Again, these are suggestions from my personal observations.

No doubt it is awkward and even invasive to make conversation due to difficult circumstances. It takes a mature person not only to make the effort, but to have the compassionate attitude of an encourager.

The best I can give you for topics of conversation, is to find subjects that are not directly related, to the issue that the person you wish to help is dealing with. Let me remind you as stated in the Don'ts chapter, don't be the aggressor; let them lead the topics of conversation if possible.

If money issues are the problem, talk about current events, family, sports, past happy memories, or anything that money has little or no relevancy to. For medical or physical issues, talk about family, pleasant memories, sports, or current events. If it's about the present circumstance, let the person involved be the one to bring it up. Emotional and spiritual issues can be very touchy, and those involved can be anywhere from the one extreme to the other. It is vital we are perceptive to where they are, and especially how they may choose to understand and apply our words of encouragement.

Sometimes it's more practical to say as little as possible; being there is more important than any words spoken. If the hurting desires to talk, they will. Your selfless action of being a good listener, shows you actually care and respect the one you're there for.

Now let's take a look at a few suggestions of what you can do to encourage with the Do's list.

1. Call, send a card, or stop in–

- Showing you care is encouragement.

- Use discretion per circumstance whether to stop in or not.

- Calling ahead (for home visits) is usually appreciated.

2. Listen confidentially without interrupting–

- Sometimes just an expression of feelings to a trusted friend can be a way of healing. Interrupting is telling them you have something more important than what they are saying.

3. Invite them over or take them out for a meal–

- Loneliness and boredom continue to drown them in the thoughts of their difficult situation. It might cost time and money, but treat them as if it were you in their predicament. Being personally involved shows you care.

4.   Pray for them–

- Pray for God's will and that they can accept it as such.

- Pray in secret for them, but encourage them by letting them know you are doing so. Ask specifically what you can bring before the Lord on their behalf.

- Continue to pray on their behalf daily, weekly, monthly, or as long as it takes.

- Believe what you pray for can happen.

5.   Give them hugs or handshakes–

- Nothing says *I care about you* like an actual physical touch. Make it a firm physical touch (if suitable), not some wimpy *I-pity-you* approach. Even a hand placed on a shoulder or other appropriate location is a way to make it personal.

6.   Confirm your interest in them–

- Smile, looking directly in their eyes, letting them know it's them you are thinking about. Say, "I care about" or "I love you." A few encouraging words go a loooong way.

7. Allow them to grieve–

- We are made with emotions and need to express them. This is part of the healing process. The times of emotional stress are when we make important decisions concerning our maturity. Allow them to use you as an unconditional shoulder to lean on.

8. Relief please–

- Discouragement comes when we can't seem to change our environment. Everybody needs a change of pace once in a while, just to renew or refresh their outlook. The difficult issue here, is if we have a lack of money or are physically unable to move into different surroundings, we remain in our familiar stagnant environment, keeping us from being stimulated by outside sources. Try to find a way to change the environment to something positive or different, regardless of how temporary.

- To the hurting I bluntly say you need not feel guilty for it. It is for nothing short of trying to have a better outlook on life. You are trying to get out of the rut of despair. Don't think for a second that because you are in a negative situation you need to act like it. Take advantage of opportunities when the door opens!

- This suggestion lies heavy on the one who comes beside for two simple reasons. The one suffering may not be able to implement it, and it's very possible that they may not even be capable at this time to think beyond the present conditions. They really do need your help so don't let them down. Again, picture yourself in their place and react accordingly.

9. Make yourself available–

*   If you are too busy wrapped up in your own little world, it makes it rather difficult to help others. Giving of your time, shows the hurting both your humility and their importance. Missed opportunities cannot be gotten back when it fits our schedules.

Dos and Don'ts P.S.

There are other aspects of the Dos and Don'ts that may seem unnecessary to some but really need to be stated. Again, this book is to help those on both sides to be as effective as possible and not waste good intentions. Giving anonymously is a great way to help and is greatly appreciated. I do wish to address some issues that some may not think about in using this method. Please don't misunderstand my intent to the point of not doing anything; by all means, do whatever you feel is right to help those you love when life happens to go sour.

Generic questions will get generic answers, and it can bring frustration to the hurting instead of helping them. If you genuinely desire to come beside and help but don't know the how or what, be honest. Tell the hurting you are willing, but don't know what to do. Again they will not be offended by your honesty and will probably open up more because of it, and more so if you have a good relationship with them.

- If you wish to donate (a meal, food items, basic everyday needs, or special gifts) it is helpful to speak to the recipient before doing so. I know this is awkward, and if you are not comfortable with the idea, it's okay. Proceed with your original plan.

- Someone might receive four meals in a row to feed four people when they may be eating alone, and it's possible (hush the thought) they might not like what you took the effort and time to make. One may unknowingly give something full of sugar to a diabetic, or possibly produce an allergic reaction due to an ingredient in the donated dish. Don't misinterpret; the gestures are more appreciated than the gift itself, because it shows care and concern. I am only pointing out how at times, due to miscommunication, efforts can be misplaced and even misunderstood.

- It is not wrong, and they won't be offended by you asking when or how much, or if there is something they don't like or presently need. You place them in an uncomfortable position if they end up throwing something away for whatever reason, especially when you ask them if they liked it.

- It is very possible when you ask them for the when, or what, they will give a generic answer. Actually you should expect it. Don't give up so easily, again they will not be offended. They are only saying what they are because, first they are not sure if you are serious, and second as a recipient they are humiliated by receiving anything, thus they feel it wrong to make any request of your generosity. In the end they will be grateful for your insight.

- Number eight on the Don't list was "Don't ask 'What can I do for you?'" Now you're asking how to implement what was just stated in conjunction with the last paragraph. Go with a specific item. Let them know you wish to bring a meal; then ask for specifics or, if it is a food shower, ask for a list of things they could use.

- Gift Cards are difficult to discuss because nobody in their right mind is going to turn that away. Generally they are a great idea, and a way to say, "I care" while remaining anonymous.

- Gift cards are also always specific. I'm not talking about the dollar amounts, but the locations of spend ability. The down side of a gift card is the different spending habits between the donor and the recipient.

- The donor may use a specific store the recipient never goes to or does not have easy access to, particularly distance. The easier you make it for the hurting in times of difficulty the more appreciated it is.

- There can be a very positive side of the gift card also. Most cards are for gas or food stores, these are for the basics of life. Periodically one may be received for a restaurant, coffee shop, clothing store, or some other luxury beyond the basic everyday needs category. Yes we all need the basics, but the-beyond-the-basics are morale boosters. They can change the environment similar to what was suggested earlier.

- The gift card also has a hidden benefit. It shows the receiver you thought about them, and cared enough to make a special effort of going somewhere to purchase the card. An action that costs time gives encouragement to the recipient, because of the personal effort it required.

When it comes to money, and the management of it for someone dealing with financial difficulties, we have a tendency to judge. It may be subconsciously, but we still form a personal opinion categorizing the person involved. When it comes to an accident, sickness, or disease, we generally just accept it because that's the way it is. Whoever is involved probably had no choice. With money, it's a completely different set of rules.

We believe the persons involved somehow let things slip or evolve into the present condition, so it's their own fault. This is entirely possible; however as was previously stated, one may have had some physical issue or accident causing a stress on their personal finances, or they may be a victim of some other circumstance.

Anonymous giving sometimes makes it easier on both parties involved, due to feelings of obligation, motivation, and even possible judging. My personal opinion is that unearned money should always be received anonymously, making God the only choice for praise and thankfulness from the receiver.

Be aware that the person receiving the monies is not ignorant of the judging, or the way others perceive them in their condition. They are just like you, except that they happen to be on the needing help side of the issue at this time. Hopefully, you now understand why and how the receiver may react and how others influence their decisions.

All that aside, God wants us to love each other unconditionally. How somebody got to where they are, or how they feel is the right way to make adjustments, is between God and that person. Both sides need to have the right motivation and be good stewards, without judging the other.

Those are a few personal observations to help the hurting and to give the helper insight. If you are one of the hurting, I sincerely hope someone will implement these principles into your life by coming alongside for comfort, support, and encouragement.

If at this time in your own life you are one of the fortunate ones to have things going well, I encourage you to seek out someone less fortunate and practice these principles. Someday, you may be the one needing help or encouragement. It's really not a secret that we ultimately all depend on someone for something during our lifetime.

You may desire to take some of my observations with a grain of salt, and I accept that. However, the issue I will not compromise on, is that God's word is the final authority. I make mistakes but God does not, so I encourage you to seek his will and direction for your life through his word. Second Timothy 2:15: "Do your best to present yourself to God as one approved, a workman who does not need to be ashamed, and who correctly handles the word of truth."

Hurting people need to know and experience that someone genuinely cares and is willing to take personal action to show it. Talk is cheap, but time and personal sacrifice speak volumes! Treat others as you wish to be treated.

Adjustments

We live in an imperfect world. I hardly need to elaborate on that statement, as everybody reading this will automatically sigh a big *Don't I know it*. The one and only reason we have hurts, problems, difficulties, and other frustrations to deal with during our time here on earth, is because of the sin curse!

My personal desire is to encourage and inform all who read this book how valuable they are. You are not set aside by what life brings. You are special and have a purpose for being where you are.

Although we may have a hard time with the concept, here is the honest truth: all of us by nature are sinful, self indulgent, prideful humans. If we can comprehend this concept, we can begin to understand the why, pertaining to the hurts we find ourselves subjected to in life. Not every hurt or difficulty that comes along is because you did something wrong and are being judged or disciplined. Remember the first statement: we live in an imperfect world.

God's Word is absolute and true; it's always relevant and never changes. He talks extensively of the constant spiritual warfare that is happening on this earth for control of our thoughts, attitudes, motivation, and personal agendas. Below are a few things for each of us to look at in our own lives. Hopefully, with wisdom and the right perspective, decisions can and will be made to move beyond your present situation of difficulty.

1. When you are humbled by your circumstances, you learn quickly why not to judge others. Before being there yourself, you could not fully understand. To pass judgment, one must know every detail of what may have happened to bring someone else to their life-altering circumstance. If you did know and understand, you probably would have an attitude of compassion rather than of judgment. An example of this may be of one being childless; only another childless couple can fully relate to the emotions and disappointments involved. God also tells us in Matthew 7:2, "For in the same way you judge others you will be judged, and with the measure you use it will be measured to you." Consider your motivation before passing judgment.

2. Harboring bitterness, envy, or anger, tends to hurt our personal relationships. Rarely does anyone want to hang around a negative person for very long. Seldom does anything good come from hanging onto negative feelings. These particular types of emotions eat us up from the inside only hurting ourselves, not the ones who are the subject of our selfish or envious attitude. These attitudes tend to wear us down physi-

cally and stress us out emotionally, causing additional problems by placing strain on other areas of our lives.

3.	Comparing ourselves to others is taking our eyes off God. Nobody wants to hear something convicting, but truth never changes. We are self-centered by nature, and it's a constant spiritual battle for control. God is not a respecter of persons; in other words, he doesn't compare you to your neighbor or friends. It does not matter to him what your position is, whom you are related to, how much money you have, or what your status in society is. If we took the challenge of not being a respecter of persons like Christ, we just might live differently. We should not be comparing ourselves to others but loving and caring for each other as we walk through life together. Don't dwell on comparing yourself to others; it only allows opportunity for dissatisfaction or envy to dominate.

4.	The definition of *a god* is anything that dominates us. God, the real one who created all things seen and unseen, gave us a commandment in Exodus chapter 20 that states: "Thou shalt have no other gods before me." So the question is, what is a god to you? What do you pursue? One can tell a person's priorities by the way they spend their time and money. It is not necessarily both time and money, because one may be correctly prioritized while the other selfishly overindulged in. God is very specific with his command when he says, "no other god." If we have anything that comes before him, we have in a sense, rejected God or given him at best second place. Anything does not only include things or objects we see, but also things unseen like a friendship, pride in ourselves, a job, or an activity.

5. It doesn't seem like it now, but this life is temporary. Therefore, it is of utmost importance we keep our eyes on the future or things we believe are to come (it's called hope). We probably have all heard the expression: "Life is like a roll of toilet paper—the closer we get to the end, the faster it goes." That may be somewhat of a funny analogy, but most adults would tend to agree it's more realistic than they care to express. Again, it depends on where you are in relation to something. If we see an airplane in the sky, it seems small, but if we are standing right next to it, we wonder how something so big can get off the ground. The big picture is simply that life is short; however, when living one day at a time with our limited viewpoint, we have the tendency to relate only to the present situation of what's here and now.

6. You are not the first person to suffer this kind of pain. Throughout history, we can find examples of someone who has endured the same or similar misunderstanding, injustice, disaster, rejection, hurts, pains, loneliness, humiliation, despair, and other emotions that accompany life's uncomfortable detours. Those areas of negativisms have not changed since the beginning of time, but are prevalent in our present world also.

7.	Never give up. I know it's not the first time you have ever heard that. You are probably already on the defensive, muttering under your breath, *It's not quite that easy.* I know and understand better than I can express in a few words on a page. Sorrow, pain, frustration, and disappointment are all part of life, but so are contentment, endurance, perseverance, joy, and peace.

Yes, I know the seven items mentioned above are blunt words, but I suggest making the necessary adjustments in life. It shows humility, character, and maturity. The evidence of what we believe to be true, comes out in our decisions and actions.

We all have ambitions or goals in life, but the real question for all of us to answer is *what do we want to be remembered for when the temporary journey on this earth is complete?* I want to give you three things to ponder.

1.	Status–There are many worthy people who hold a position of status and are used for the progress or benefit of many other people. Status is not wrong if used for the correct reasons. It is a responsibility and should be considered a privilege to influence for the benefit of others. However, status can be abused, such as someone who has the wrong attitude by taking advantage of those under their authority simply because their abilities or position allow them to.

2. Satisfaction—Another word may be contentment. Again, these words and their meanings are not wrong; as a matter of fact, they are usually associated with the good or positive things in life that bring fulfillment. The dominant question at this point would be *what is satisfaction?* My handy dictionary tells me it is a *feeling of pleasure or happiness when a need or desire is fulfilled.* It may be our own needs or even for someone else's that we had the opportunity to be part of. So it all goes back to the why we are in pursuit of something, our motivation, what we expect or feel we deserve, and how to use the resources given to us. Those resources may be anything from financial or physical, to comforting words spoken in love, for the emotional or spiritual needs of people God has placed in your life.

3. Stuff—Just the word *stuff* generates many thoughts; we all have ideas what stuff is and how it affects us. Material stuff, the objects used to help us live life, can be used for selfish reasons or to aid us in building relationships. Sometimes the information highway uploads unneeded stuff into our minds, keeping us from thinking for ourselves. Then there is the stuff of daily living bogging us down, making our lives so busy we don't have or allow time for God or others. Stuff can be just that, stuff or filler, something to just take up our time and energy while draining us from being productive in constructive ways. Stuff can be

prioritized for our own benefit of usefulness as well as those whom we have relationships with.

It does me no good to elaborate further on these issues; I'm sure you have already placed yourself somewhere in the context of these three words and their influences on your personal life. If you have read through these words and mentally thought of how they fit others, I strongly encourage you to reread through them, this time with yourself as the main character.

The *me* attitude gets in the way. We all have a tendency to try to hold onto something called control. We hate the idea of losing control because it might force us to deal with possible changes in our familiar and comfortable world. Proverbs 3:5–6 says, "Trust in the Lord with all your heart and lean not on your own understanding. In all your ways acknowledge him, and he will make your paths straight."

Trust is having confidence in or relying on something or someone to take responsibility for your benefit. Those two verses work together. If we truly trust God (whatever our situation), we want him to direct our paths. Again, that can only happen if we have a relationship with him. Psalms 37:23–24 are follow-ups that encourage us to pursue God's way. "If the Lord delights in a man's way, he makes his steps firm, though he stumbles, he will not fall, for the Lord upholds him with his hand."

I get excited when I read encouraging words like that. Just knowing God cares enough to protect me in those times of disillusion and uncertainty causes me to smile.

If you have accepted God's word as truth, you know he will never let you down. Adjustments in life are usually hard, and when we deal with it alone, it only seems to multiply the frustrations. Accept the changes, give God the burden, and allow others to be your support.

Misery loves company—there is more truth in that small phrase than most of us would admit. The real question is *why?* Probably because it gives comfort to the one in misery, just knowing someone else is feeling the same pain. They find comfort knowing they are not isolated from the rest of society because of their difficulty. Having someone to cry with or relate to in our down times can ease the feelings of loneliness that usually come with unexpected detours in life. Companionship, someone to share with or a listening ear for support, thus making things easier.

Jesus tells us he is there, as in Matthew 11:28–30: "Come to me all you who are weary and burdened, and I will give you rest. Take my yoke upon you and learn from me, for I am gentle and humble in heart, and you will find rest for your souls. For my yoke is easy and my burden is light." Notice we need to take action, and the result should be for us to learn from him; then we will have the desired rest or peace. He does not say the problems will just disappear, but he does promise to be a comfort to us during these times.

What a picture of being there for a brother or sister in time of need! Right beside them, taking part of the load, not pushing or pulling like we sometimes tend to do, but right beside, sharing the burden equally. Anybody that has had help, knows the load shared, is easier bared.

Personal Conflict

Just living seems to bring issues of chaos without explanation, including conflict, disagreement, restlessness, and struggles for peace, even when we desire to live a quiet, non-conflict lifestyle.

When there is a fight or battle, it's usually for the underlying reason of power, the ability to control, or to have dominance. This principle is true in both the physical and nonphysical realms. We know from history that the battles or difficulties in life shape us in multiple ways. We learn from them, are strengthened through them, and hopefully make adjustments because of them.

Living on this earth is the only requirement needed to be a participant in the battle of control. By nature, we look out for ourselves; most personal decisions made revolve around where we fit in and how it benefits us.

Just as we change physically when we age, the same should be true emotionally and spiritually. We are not all going to be facing the same trial, hurt or uncertainty, but what these difficult times do is the same for all. Life is a journey of growing or maturing in relationships, faith, and hope.

Most of us would rather plead ignorance, desiring to live a peaceful, undisturbed life. As much as we wish to avoid conflict, we must acknowledge we are involved in a war! The battle is for control of our minds, will, and the priorities that shape our lives.

As stated previously, the one and only reason we deal with hurts, difficulties, problems, misunderstandings, sorrow, pain, disorder, and negative situations, is because of the sin curse on the earth we inhabit. Everything in life is subject to this principle, and that is the reason we deal with the struggles we do.

I cannot write what life is about without getting to the basics of what life is. I personally believe we are only on this earth temporarily, but that we live forever. I believe the real reason we are given the opportunity to live on earth is to choose or reject God. Life is about choices of priorities; the difficulties, pain, and hurts of living, are the tools used to force us into making the decisions that shape our true priorities or convictions.

This battle for the mind is a spiritual one, personally fought by everybody every day. It is a relentless, life-long struggle of being prepared, being on guard, and engaging the enemy (evil) with outcomes and results that stand for all of eternity.

In the spiritual battle that is taking place in the unseen world all around us, we need not only be aware of who we are, but also who the enemy is and what's at stake. There is God, Satan the deceiver, and you—the one both desire to have allegiance from. God in his wisdom has given each of us a free will, to choose whom we will serve and commit ourselves to.

Presently, you are asking what this has to do with hurting people. Let me explain. Because of the sin-filled world in which we live, there is pain, sorrow, tears, and finally, death. Those are the results of the sin curse on this earth. Revelation 21:1 tells us, "There will be a new heaven and a new earth, for the first heaven and the first earth shall pass away." Then in verse four it says, "There will be no more death, or mourning, or crying, or pain, for the old order of things has passed away."

Hallelujah, I can't help but get excited! It only stands to reason that if there is no more sorrow, pain, crying, or death, then all our trials, difficulties, and negative circumstances will also come to an end forever! That's good news, and it gives hope to endure the present situations, knowing God has already won the battle through the sacrifice of Jesus Christ on the cross.

The tragedy here is for those who have not acknowledged God as their redeemer. The promise of all things new is only for those who have accepted God's gift of salvation. The rest will never experience an end to the pain and sorrow of life, even death will not end it. If you're not sure where you stand with your creator, find a Bible and read Romans 10:9–10. It's worth your eternity!

It may be hard to look beyond where you are at this very moment, because life still needs to be lived in this present environment. Informed people can make informed choices, so let's look at some of the major facts of what we need to deal with on a daily basis. Then, hopefully we can rise above whatever keeps us from being productive in this life by making wise, informed decisions.

As a reminder of what we are dealing with, I point out Ephesians 6:12: "For our struggle is not against flesh and blood, but against the rulers, against the authorities, against the powers of this dark world and against the spiritual forces of evil in the heavenly realms." As believers in Christ, we are fighting an unseen battle for the mind and the will. The seen things and life on this earth are the battlefield and weapons used to play it out.

Listed below are issues and participants in the spiritual battle we are subjected to daily.

- Who We Are:
  » A living soul, created to live eternally. A temporary resident on this earth. Made up of a body, mind, and soul.

- What we should do:
  » Acknowledge him (God our creator) in all our ways, do all things unto him and not unto man, seek his will. Praise him and thank him. Seek forgiveness when we let him down.

- Who God Is:
  » King of kings, Savior, Redeemer, Friend of sinners, The I Am that I Am, The living God that was and is and is to come, Lord, Christ, Messiah, Sovereign, Holy, Just, Father of light, Alpha and Omega, Divine Authority, Judge, Creator of all things,

Emanuel, Jehovah, Rabbi, Teacher, Master, Shepherd, Prince of Peace.

- What he does:
  - » Loves us unconditionally. Provides for our daily needs and protects us. Is preparing a place in eternity for believers, controls all things, strengthens us, forgives and forgets our sins if we confess them. Gives grace and mercy. Never changes.

- Who Satan Is:
  - » Deceiver, father of lies, adversary, tempter, serpent, prince of darkness, ruler of this world, accuser of the brethren, author of confusion.

- What he tries to do:
  - » Keep us so busy we do not have time for a relationship with God. Puts things like: Comparisons, doubt, fear, worry, anxiety, bitterness, envy, jealousy, loneliness, lust, despair, and self-pity in our minds. Tells us to blame someone else or even God when life falls apart. He wants us to fail in our relationship with God. Make us believe we are self-sufficient. Tells us that sin is fun but fails to let us know the consequences.

Jesus paid our sin debt on the cross, already defeating Satan. Consequently, Satan's alternative plan is to cause as much damage as possible to God's creation. He wants to destroy you because, if he can't do anything to God, he wants to destroy the one thing that has the most value to God—you!

The list above gives a brief overview of who God and Satan are. The way they think and act out their character is completely opposite of each other. God is truth and peace; Satan is lies and chaos.

The first thing we tend to do when things don't go as we had hoped or expected, and certainly when the bottom falls out on our lives, is to blame God. We need to start thinking in another direction, because the best thing we could do for ourselves is run *to* God, not *from* him. He is the only one who genuinely cares about us with the ability and resources to actually do something.

We need to have the right mindset by submitting to the understanding that everything is done according to God's will and for his glory, accepting that what he has decided is best for us.

So what happens when we indulge in comparisons, selfishness, or wrong attitudes? Is that the way to escape our troubles, change our circumstances, or fix the problem?

The truth is, we all like a pity party once in a while, and I'll be the first to admit it. Somehow we justify self-pity by telling ourselves we are comfortable staying down, instead of trying to get back up. Everybody knows it's a lot easier falling down than it is getting up, especially when you keep getting hit over and over again. Sometimes we just want to be left alone, desiring to crawl someplace where nobody can find us, a place to hide from trouble where we can feel comfortable and in control, without being made to feel guilty or judged by our peers.

Life is challenging enough when things are normal, if there is such a thing. Often we find ourselves doing what we don't want to do, being where we don't want to be, or dealing with circumstances with which we would rather have never been involved. Even if it was completely beyond our control in the first place, we tend to blame ourselves and even resort to self-pity. It's easy to ask *Why me* and maybe even easier to come up with many reasons to justify the why not.

More times than not, we pray and pray and pray about something, but grow weary and are disappointed when nothing happens in a timely manner. We have all heard the religious, biblical answer to this dilemma: God answers in three ways: yes, no, or wait. Sometimes it's rather difficult to understand, or even believe God has a plan, and that what we are enduring is part of it. We have our own plans or ideas of not only how things should progress, but the timing in which it should happen.

Take a step back by remembering two things: one is that all things work for the glory of God. The other is that our timing is usually not God's timing. I wish to highlight what happened in Daniel's life when he prayed, why his prayer was heard, and even how timing was an issue. Read the two verses below and place yourself and your situation into the scenario. In the spiritual battle, we need to have the right relationship and motivation for the right outcome.

Daniel 10:12–13, "Do not be afraid, Daniel. Since the first day that you set your mind to gain understanding and to humble yourself before God, your words were heard, and I have come in response to them. But the prince of the Persian kingdom resisted me twenty-one days. Then, Michael, one of the chief princes, came to help me because I was detained."

The word *battle* indicates many participates, but at times, it feels you are the only one wrestling with the choices that need to be made during unwanted circumstances. Keep your focus correct. Look beyond yourself.

Self-pity is not a good character builder. Take the emphasis off the negative and place it on the positive. Be thankful. When life bottoms out, the farthest thing from our mind is being thankful. God reveals and encourages us in James 1:2: "Consider it pure joy when you face trials." *Joy* means *happiness* or *pleasure*. It's not the trial we desire but the result of the trial. James finishes by telling us the eventual reward is maturity. I can't imagine anybody wanting to be treated as a child their entire life, but rather would want to fit into society and be able to experience the benefits and privileges of an adult.

Being thankful is an expression of gratitude or appreciation for something done on our behalf. The expression can be in the form of acknowledgement for something or an unselfish act someone did on our behalf.

One way we express ourselves is to verbally speak our thanks. Another way is to give something of ourselves, showing our gratitude for the act of kindness someone has bestowed upon us. An attitude of gratitude is a solid step in the right direction. Thankfulness is usually a character trait of who we are.

Thankfulness takes the spotlight off us, and gives meaning to life due to an outside influence. It is impossible to be thankful without thinking of who is responsible for our thankfulness. A pleasant memory can cause a smile due to joy the thing or person we are thankful for brings to our attention. Possibly a sunny day, children, grandchildren, a kind word, a card, time with friends, smells, sounds—the list is inexhaustible.

If we actually took the time to concentrate on just the things we take for granted each day, we might be humbly surprised. We don't appreciate some things until they are taken away. Be thankful for what you have now; thankfulness is a positive emotion that encourages and changes perspective.

I get excited when I think of things to be thankful for. I'm going to bring a few more things to your attention, just to get you thinking about how we forget and take things for granted.

God gave us five senses to use, and they each bring us pleasure in different ways. The eyes help us navigate when walking, they allow us to see God's creation, and guide us in many aspects of life. Our noses allow us to identify smells, keeping us from danger as well as giving pleasure. The ability to touch and feel things aids us in ways beyond the actual touch. Hearing is communication and understanding of whatever or whoever is near us; sounds can give warning or direction. Speaking is also communication, especially the connection with another person, and singing can be part of the speech sense. So often we forget the benefits of music, and the joy or comfort it brings regardless of where we are in life.

All of these senses can bring pain and pleasure, or bring about information to make decisions that directly effect who we are. These God-given abilities also involve emotions that help us relate to those around us. Those are just five things we can be thankful for in life, and there are so many more.

Being thankful is only one way to open a door to the positive, bringing self-instigated encouragement. I suggest another challenge for certain reinforcement: pray for other people. Yes, you are going through maybe some of the toughest things no human should have to endure. Look beyond yourself for just a moment and maybe, just maybe, someone else is going through something of equal difficulty and needs your prayers and encouragement.

Prayer not only brings someone else's name and circumstance before our creator, but puts you in God's presence at the same time. A truly thankful person is a giving person. I'm not necessarily talking about money; giving means to let someone have something you own or control. It may be your time, resources, or abilities. Giving may even involve putting someone else's problems before your own. Thankfulness can only come from the heart; more than likely, that heart has grown to understand what being thankful is because of those trying times in life. Nobody relates to someone suffering, except one who is, or has gone through something similar.

So when fighting the daily battle of the will, remember who you are, and that the decisions today stand for all of eternity. Don't forget to spend time daily in God's Word and in prayer, so you are equipped to fight the battles of life.

Do your research, know the enemy, ask for help, do what you know is right, don't dwell on the negative, and fight with confidence because of who you are!

Perspective

We need to take a look at perspective because it has more influence than any of us care to admit.

Perspective is a *measured assessment of a situation.* *Measured assessment,* broken down, translates to a *comparison.* The first place any human naturally goes when comparing is to another human, evaluating what the differences are between them. Basically, we come to one of three conclusions:

1. I am better

2. We are similar or the same

3. They are better

These conclusions can be drawn from either the people involved or from life's circumstances. In a perfect world numbers one and three simply would not exist.

When we compare ourselves with others, we can always find someone to fit the particular criteria we desire. We make ourselves believe we are better or worse than they are to achieve the outcome we subconsciously have predetermined. Let's look at how these stack up in life's circumstances.

As previously mentioned, we will all go through some kind of trial or unpleasant time during our lifetime. These times are what make us who we are, not only giving the influences or criteria that force us to make choices, but refining and defining us by those choices.

Comparison can be either a dangerous or a commendable way of sizing up our true values, depending on what we are comparing to and the reasons we draw a conclusion. Drawing conclusions for the right reasons helps us make wise and useful decisions, pertaining to the handling of whatever the particular situation is. It's easy to use a comparison to achieve any self-motivated results, which is what our human tendency wants to do. We may choose something or someone that elevates us or puts us in a better light. However in doing so, we have only lied to ourselves, and will never be able to make the necessary adjustments to overcome, simply because we have not convinced ourselves we need to change or adapt.

However, the opposite can also be true. We pick a comparison that looks better than us or where we are, lowering our self worth or self esteem, believing that it's not worth the energy it might take to improve. Again, we have only misled ourselves with this kind of mentality.

The next question is hanging heavy. Do we always need to change? Let me rephrase it so the question is aimed directly at each one of us. Are you comfortable in times of difficulty? Are you satisfied with where you are and willing to accept what your life has become? Hopefully you have answered both questions in your mind before you read the conclusion that I have drawn from my own struggles. I perceive you are not comfortable, and if you are, do you not wish to continuously improve? So yes, you do need to change. The reason change is required regardless of where you are, is because life is a process of maturing.

Society moves forward and develops new things that help us meet our daily needs. We have gone from outhouses to indoor plumbing, horse and buggy to cars, and from pencil and paper to computers. Just like society changes to benefit mankind, we also need to change our personal lives to mature. Not too many people want to go back to the old ways; we should think of our personal life in the same sense, when it comes to relationships and personal growth.

Then, you may ask, does anyone ever mature to the point of being comfortable in life's uncontrollable situations? Again I remind you, life is a process of maturing that ends only in death. So even if it does get easier to handle things with maturity, we still feel sorrow, disappointment, pain, and the other negative aspects of life in this sin-filled environment.

Getting back to the idea of perspective or comparison: What should we be comparing our lives and its circumstances to? Should it be to other people? No, simply because people change. At certain times, you may be looking good compared to somebody, and yet at some other point in life, you may not measure up to the same person.

God is the standard, the only one we can depend on as the perfect example through Jesus Christ. He never changes and I'm so thankful he doesn't; otherwise, where is our hope? With Christ as our example of comparison, we get a glimpse of our shortcomings and begin to understand why it's an ongoing endeavor.

An example to help understand perspective is to revert back to your childhood. Remember the yard or playground where you used to play when growing up? It seemed big enough at the time because of your size, and it was all you really knew. Now when you visit the same yard or playground as an adult, it probably seems small in comparison to how you remembered it as a child. That's because you are bigger now. It's not that the play area had become smaller, but the fact that you have grown.

Another example from our childhood to adulthood may be one of a school bully who seemed overwhelming and scary, but when you run into that same person today, they may seem smaller and less intimidating because both of you have changed. Maybe an adult you once knew to be strong and healthy has aged or been sick to the point of frailty; consequently, you look at them in a completely different way.

My point is this: how involved you are in something and what you are comparing it to, determines the degree of difficulty. Sometimes our circumstance may seem overwhelming and intimidating; other times we feel we can handle it. We each draw on our respective resources through friends, family, personal faith, or even our finances to give us strength or support in handling unexpected circumstances, however long, short, or difficult that may be.

One analogy I like to use to give perspective of how we see things from a limited point of view is this: Picture yourself walking alone through the woods, on a moonless night holding only a small flashlight. The light can pierce the darkness but for only a limited distance and direction. You can only make decisions for your walk based on the information gathered from what you see in that limited area.

Now picture yourself walking in the same area when the sun is directly overhead on a clear day. Even with the trees blocking some of the sun, you will be able to see clearly in all directions and for great distances. This allows you to make better decisions as to which direction to go and gives confidence in your steps. How minor and even useless is that flashlight when you have the sun to guide you? I will only use the visual analogy here, because what I want you to understand is the difference of what we see compared to what God sees.

Trials in life are similar to being alone and lost in some forest at night. Everything is unfamiliar and scary. We almost always start thinking of the worst possible outcome, believing our environment is working against us. Things we hear are multiplied in our minds because we do not understand them. Time drags as we wait in hopes of the situation turning positive.

Now think how much easier it would be if you were not alone. What if another person was with you for support, or better yet, what if there were many people with you? It should be pretty obvious that the perspective might change from discouragement to encouragement, simply because of companionship.

The same encouragement can be true in respect to seeing things clearly, just like the sunlight dispersing the darkness. The more information we have to make decisions with, the more comfortable and confident we can be in making those difficult, life-altering decisions.

One thing I can say for certain: nobody really understands the degree of hurt, misunderstanding, despair, or frustration one feels unless he has actually experienced something of the same nature or close to it. An example of this is similar to a picture of a place you have never been. You see it, but have not experienced the sounds, smells, or any other emotions that may accompany what you see in the picture.

As a child, I saw pictures of foreign countries and heard the stories of the culture differences, but until I actually took a mission trip to a third world country as a young adult, I did not fully understand or comprehend. I'll compare it to a roller coaster ride. Your friends tell you about the thrill of the first hill, how the stomach does not keep up with the rest of the body, or the feeling you might fall off the ride. Only when you have experienced the coaster's first hill yourself, can you relate to the thrill or agony it brings.

The roller coaster is another good example of the issues or hurts that life can bring. Once you are on and come over the top of the first hill, there is no getting off, and you are going for the ride, like it or not. Sometimes it's just a small roller coaster, and other times it's more than we can see, causing us to wonder if it will ever end.

Trials can have their ups and downs and occasionally a sharp curve or two, just like the roller coaster. It's good to know it will come to an end eventually; however, even after the ride is over, we still feel the effects. Just because whatever sidetracked you for whatever length of time seems done, the effects continue to have influence on us, sometimes long after the hurt is past.

Usually, difficulties, trials, or unplanned circumstances create issues we did not previously think we would need to deal with on a personal basis. We always believe it happens only to the other guy, and we act surprised when we are the ones enduring such hardships. Even if the trouble was a minor hiccup or speed bump in life, the wise realize they need to make adjustments, to allow these things and be prepared to endure. It is very possible for someone to face the same difficulty again, and possibly to a greater degree.

It only seems reasonable we cannot remain the same after enduring hardships, because we should have matured through it and changed our perspective. I'm sure someone who has lost a loved one they genuinely cared for, will have a greater compassion for someone of similar pain. They have encountered the same type of difficulty, gaining an understanding that can only be learned from experience. That's perspective.

It's been said the difference between a recession and depression depends on whether you're going through it or someone else is. Something may affect us while devastating others, such as a tornado ripping your neighbor's house apart while the only damage you received were a few windows blown out. It may only be a speed bump for you, while your neighbor is dealing with a major disruption in life.

In the realm of perspective, I wish to discuss time. Time plays a major part in how we handle issues in our lives. We are the now generation, impatient, not wanting to wait for anything. Our society has not only taught us we can have things we desire immediately, but has also provided a way for it to happen. Some examples are credit cards, fast food, ATMs, 24-hour fuel or food, the Internet (anything from information to downloading movies and online chats), microwave ovens, cell phones, and iPods; the list can go on with virtually everything instantly at our fingertips.

Nevertheless, I cannot find one time that Jesus was in a hurry during his time on earth. Everything we call logical or might feel an obligation for, seemed to have no bearing on Christ. When the crowds came to hear him speak, he left them and went away alone to pray. When he was told Lazarus was dying, he did not rush, but waited a few days actually letting him die. When the storm raged around him and his disciples, he slept in the boat.

In Samuel, we read the story of David the shepherd boy, who many years later, became king of Israel. In Genesis we have the story of Joseph, the younger brother who was sold into slavery and endured many years of uncertainty, but was eventually promoted to second-in-command of the whole land of Egypt. Many years passed, and many trials full of emotion came into the lives of these two people.

If you know the stories, you know it was not an easy road for either one of them; they probably even faced the same types of emotional anxieties to which you are subjected. God gave us these examples in history to learn from and be encouraged by.

The most important thing most of us neglect to acknowledge is that whatever takes place in our lives, just like in the lives of the biblical examples, is for the glory of God.

I'm sure when Joseph sat in the Egyptian jail, he felt like it was the end of the line for him. It looked like a hopeless situation, but we know after spending years in jail, God did have something special for him because he stayed faithful. He was placed in a position of authority, saving many people from starvation during years of famine, including his own family. Jesus himself did not start his ministry until he was thirty years old.

I point out these examples to illustrate that we may not see the *why* we are enduring this particular crisis in our life. It may be many years before we are able to use the present circumstance of learning and training. It takes many years for a fruit tree to grow from a seed into a mature, productive tree. We need to look at our trials as a time of maturing, for a future opportunity to serve God.

Training is tough; it takes discipline and stretches us beyond what we are accustomed to. Self-discipline is the most difficult because we set our own agendas and limits. When it comes to life's difficult times, we don't always see them as training. We see them as some kind of discipline or misfortune, because we did not have control of the when, how, or what.

Training comes in different forms, depending on what we are being trained for. An astronaut, banker, electrician, nurse, or fisherman each require different types of training, to be effective in their fields or lines of work. Whatever the particular issue anybody is being trained for, requires time.

Time is something we do not control. We cannot stop it, speed it up, slow it down, buy it, sell it, package it, or ignore it. Our trials, hurts, and undesirable circumstances are similar to time: we don't control them; God does. We need to allow him to be the one we depend on to take us through it.

We have all heard that anything worthwhile takes time. During our time of training, even if it's not by our own choice, we need discipline and consistency, or another way to put it, perseverance. Nobody goes into a race without knowing what or where the finish line is. Life as it happens doesn't always allow us that privilege. However, we can still set goals by making choices that keep us aimed in the right direction, regardless of what we may be facing or how long the duration of time is.

I have an example that may just help grasp a glimpse of how life might work out better for us, if we let go of the control and work with God instead of against him.

Many of us have the privilege of driving a car, and with that privilege come a few rules of the road and personal responsibilities. Those rules are for our own protection, even though we may feel they restrict our freedom. If someone decides they do not want to abide to the standard, they endanger not only themselves but others as well. If they disregard a stop sign, or drive on the wrong side of the road, they may be lucky enough to get away with it for a while, but the odds are not in their favor. Continuing to disregard the law will eventually result in an accident, ticket, jail, or possibly even death.

If a driver is caught breaking the law, they should be penalized, maybe even to the degree of losing the privilege of driving for a while. Although they may take the penalty as infringement on their rights, ultimately it is meant for good not only for them, but for others too.

God really does have our best interest in mind, even during those times we feel he has abandoned or forgotten us. We need to realize he sets limits for reasons that we cannot see or even understand.

I'm not suggesting that whatever you are going through is punishment, so please don't look at it that way. I am only suggesting you allow God to be your guide in life, especially during times of uncertainty.

I also believe we are not always enjoying the freedoms and blessings of Christ because, like the privilege of driving, we have our own ideas of how to handle things instead of trusting God. When your GPS (God) gives you directions, you may think you have a better way by choosing a shortcut that will save time, only to find out for some unexpected reason you end up backtracking, making the trip longer in the end.

If you knew the reward or blessing would equal or exceed your trial, would you have a different outlook while going through it? Galatians 6:9, "Let us not become weary in doing good, for in proper time we will reap a harvest if we do not give up." We get stuck in our narrow, limited minds, by drawing conclusions from what we see or understand. Perspective is going beyond where we are, looking at the whole picture instead of the temporary difficulty that overwhelms us. Remember, perspective is how we view life, especially our own in comparison to what we feel is right.

Intriguing Words

Words are powerful. At some point in life, we hang onto every word someone is speaking, usually because it has a direct effect on us. The initial step of understanding how certain words influence our choices, is to understand their meaning and application.

Take the word *insulate*, for instance. When something is insulated, it is protected from an outside force or environment. However, the same word can be used to describe a place or person so removed from the normal routines of life that it is almost impossible to get to it or them.

Personal barriers can sometimes keep help from reaching us when needed. Our choice of insulating ourselves as a defense could be prolonging the very situation we desire to come to completion.

Let's be honest, when we hurt emotionally, words matter! However, most words spoken to us during the down times are usually not desired or received very well. We would much rather be left alone, convinced that whoever is trying to be of some comfort to us, knows nothing of the pain we are enduring.

Hurting people can and usually do feel isolated or alone. The thought pattern is *Nobody knows how I feel, There is no hope, I can't take it, Why me? This will never end, and nobody really cares about me anyway.* Can you see by the very thoughts of someone enduring difficult times, how they might feel as the emotions run wild? Maybe you are experiencing some of these thoughts at this very moment. May I suggest you are normal?

Don't despair or give up hope. I know the next phrase seems trite, but it's true. Things will change despite the darkness that surrounds and possibly even overwhelms you right now.

In Ecclesiastes 3:1, Solomon tells us there is a time for everything and a season for every activity under heaven. In verses two through eight he continues to tell us about the different emotions and activities in life to which we are subjected. In verses nine through seventeen he comments on whom we are compared to God and what our perspective should be. I challenge you to take your Bible and read Ecclesiastes chapter three for yourself, and I also suggest you conclude the reading with Ecclesiastes 12:13–14. This is where Solomon gives the summary of the wisdom he has acquired during life.

Sometimes it helps to think about the positive things we so often take for granted. Words spark memories and can bring instant relief or joy. Let me make some suggestions that may cause you, at least for a few moments, to dwell on something other than what may be dominating your thoughts. Let your mind wander as you think about the following phrases and the calming effect they may entice. Read them slowly; allowing the thoughts to sink in:

> Lightly falling rain, freshly mown grass, flowers gently swaying in the breeze, birds singing, cloudless blue sky, the voice of a friend from far away, the smell of freshly baked bread, warm sunshine, the quietness of nature.

As your mind thought on these few things, I would hope you could see how words can be a powerful tool, influencing not only thoughts, but attitude and emotions.

Personally one of the best antidotes to keeping my sanity during many months of uncertainty has been to spend time thinking about the many taken-for-granted blessings that are part of any day. Regardless of what has transpired in your life, look for and dwell on what has previously brought joy and fulfillment into your life. Memories of good times can be a major encouragement when facing an uncertain future.

Okay, on to another word of interest. I wish to speak briefly about the meaning behind the word *tolerate*. It means *to put up with or accept, to allow*. The application pertaining to tolerating can be from both sides of the hurt. The hurting individual really doesn't want help, or possibly doesn't know how to accept it, so they tolerate it. The helping partner is likewise not sure how to help or feels obligated to be there, so they also tolerate being there.

There is no benefit in tolerating. It's like spending an evening with someone and neither of you speaking. Yes, you are together, and maybe that chases some of the loneliness or boredom away, but relationships take involvement, and communication is a major part of the connection. Communication is deeper than just being there or saying the right words; it is a compassion for the other person, with a desire to be the encouragement needed.

Hopefully you are able to make a connection on the same level, and help each other understand the feelings, emotions, questions, hopes, fears, or other issues that become relevant. The ultimate goal is that both sides willingly pursue working together for the best possible outcome. Maybe that's why God allowed the situation to occur in the first place, so **both** of you can learn and mature through it.

If you are one who has already experienced a situation and are aware of a brother or sister going through something similar, I believe God gives you the special privilege and responsibility of being the one to come alongside. In Matthew 25:40, Jesus declared: "Whatever you did for one of the least of these brothers of mine, you did for me."

Following are a few other words to elaborate on, that seem to be key issues when it comes to the hurts of life. They are *judged, self-esteem, dependent, worry*, and *contentment.*

Judged

The word *judged* brings a shudder to most people. We do not relish having others evaluate our lives, and then draw their own opinionated conclusions as to whether or not we have made the right decisions, about how to live. Judged, is one major aspect of how most people feel when going through life's difficulties.

If you are the helper, this is the most important word to keep in mind as a central focus while dealing with the hurting. Your words and your actions need to portray that you are not there to judge, but to come alongside and encourage. This is probably the biggest hinge point of winning their trust and being able to be part of the healing process. If you miss this important relationship-building tool, everything else will be surface quality only, because the hurting will write you off immediately.

To grasp my point, we must first understand what a *judge* is. A *judge* is *one who has supreme authority to evaluate something such as a situation, character, contest, performance, behavior, or some competition, to conclude one final verdict or decision from multiple possibilities.* The way for a judge to draw the correct conclusion or verdict is to see the whole picture with all the information and possibilities, before making an informed decision according to the laws or rules pertaining to the issue involved.

Why do we feel judged? Could it be because things did not work out as we planned, so we immediately pass judgment on ourselves? We believe we have not been playing according to the rules and somehow cheated, or that we took a shortcut and now are reaping our just reward. We reap what we sow; consequently, we must have done something wrong to bring this particular situation upon ourselves. We feel responsible for whatever we may have been involved in.

Then we go the next step, beating ourselves up with personal evaluations or scenarios of what it was we did wrong. Sometimes it is of our own doing; we need not only be aware of that possibility, but humble enough to admit it, asking for forgiveness and accepting the consequences of our actions.

Besides self-judging, we judge others. Before we do that, we need to ask ourselves a few questions. Do I know all the facts? Am I an expert in this area? Do I have the right? What if someone were judging me for something similar? I submit we stop spending our time and energy judging; instead we should make an effort to help.

Self Esteem

A factor that tops the chart in a hurting person's life is self esteem. When the plans we make and the goals we set come to a screeching halt because of some uncontrollable event, we have a natural tendency to look at ourselves as the main reason for the failure. It does not matter if it did or did not directly involve choices we made. We take it personally and find a reason to blame ourselves.

Regardless of how we got to the point of judging ourselves for shortcomings and personal failures, we feel responsible. If we can't control our own life, we feel like useless pawns, convincing ourselves we are of no value, and therefore can't contribute anything positive to the world around us. Soon we quit trying, and adopt the attitude of worthlessness to society.

Personal value comes from seeing who we are from God's point of view. Sometimes we make ourselves valuable by the world's standards because of what we accomplish in society. Be it money, power, or status, our value is based only on the latest accomplishment. We are all subject to losing this kind of self worth at a moment's notice. From the top there is plenty of room to fall, whether it is disrespect, personal humility, a lack of followers, or a loss of ability to persuade others we have the right answers. Culture tells us our personal value comes from where we are in society, therefore giving us value or self worth by comparison.

Our real value comes from who we are, not what we do, have, or what others think. An interesting phase I have heard is: We are or become what we think others think we are. That statement bothers me, simply because if it were true, we have only assumed our identity according to what society allows us to be.

Our identity should be based on where we came from: our creator, God! Our value is priceless. Each of us is unique and important as an individual. If someone is dedicated to your well-being, and cares about every aspect of your life, it doesn't take long for you to start believing it to the point of having self worth. God cares for you, and the people around you are the individuals God is using to show his love and concern for you personally.

Dependent

Nobody likes needing to depend on someone else to meet their basic needs of survival. We are naturally wired to be self-sufficient, independent, and in control of our own destiny. If we rely on others, we feel they are in control, dominating our lives, making decisions that directly affect who we are. We somehow get the idea that we will become what they want us to be, losing our own identity.

Maybe this is the reason we fight so hard, trying to maintain stability in our lives when it is disrupted by unexpected circumstance. We are full of pride—we sometimes call it *integrity* so we don't feel guilty. We think being dependent exposes us as weak or below those around us. The opportunity we miss when we are absorbed in the attitude of *poor me,* is that others are not only able, but willing to help us in difficult times.

Being dependent can have its rewards. Accept it; you may be pleasantly surprised. Maybe the one who comes along to help has some insight to expedite your recovery. What an opportunity to be a good example and possibly influence your helper in positive ways. You may also gain a friend through this whole ordeal.

Worry

Most people shy away from the word *worry,* because it has a guilt factor attached. We all have been taught it is wrong to worry, and that by doing so we are not being spiritual. Let's be realistic; all normal people worry about something at some time. I'm not trying to justify it, but simply acknowledging worry as an emotion we entertain during times of uncertainty. We don't know how things may turn out, and as time or resources are running out, we begin to expect the worst. We start thinking the opportunity for improvement has vanished, especially when our prayers have seemingly gone unanswered.

Yes, it is true worrying over something never changes it, and giving it totally to God is the right answer. There is a fine line between running through the possible solutions and worrying. Our prayers should be for God's will, but we do not always know what that is, especially compared to what we believe the best answer is. God gave us the ability to think and make decisions and wants us to do so, but we must be careful not to cross over into the area of distress and anxiety. These are nothing less than symptoms of trying to take control of something we have no authority, ability, or right to.

Contentment

Contentment is being satisfied with the way things are, happy and accepting of a situation or course of action. Not wanting to change anything from its present state. Satisfied.

Everybody desires contentment. Isn't this what man longs for? We pursue it in many different ways, always trying to fill some personal desire to give us the feeling we have arrived. Contentment can only come from within; nobody else can decide for us if we are willing to accept things like they are in our lives.

God created families with the idea of the parents taking the responsibility for teaching and providing the basic needs of their children. Therefore, if we are under the watchful eye of God our father and he has our best interest in mind, shouldn't we be content, leaving no place for worry and anxiety? I know those are strong words, and I wrestle with this concept just as much as you do. We all want the peace but have a hard time giving up the worry.

If nothing else has been learned by my own experience through the loss of income, it is that I can be very satisfied with a lot less of the materialistic possessions in life. When we strip away all the extra busyness in life and get down to the basics, we find where our real values lie. To help you grasp an understanding of this, I will use an example that may not be so pleasant to some, but is very direct in helping us better understand real value.

When we are healthy, we set priorities as to what is important and how we spend our time and resources; but have you ever been so sick it consumes every part of your body? When that happens, you can think of nothing else. It doesn't matter if the lawn gets mowed, the dishes washed, or if you look presentable to anybody. You don't care about anything except feeling better. Priorities change and the priorities we might normally see as having value, lessen in comparison to the present circumstance. What are the issues in your life keeping you from being content, happy, and satisfied?

Paul said in Philippians 4:11, "For I have learned to be content whatever the circumstances." I wish to point out Paul said he *learned*; it didn't just happen. I'm sure he had a few difficulties in life that brought him to that point. We too must learn through our own not-so-pleasant experiences to find contentment, in what is of real value to us.

Nutshell

In our own demanding world of getting what we want or need in days, hours, or minutes, I wish I could give you just a few right-to-the-point, waste-no-time nuggets of advice. However, as has been stated many times throughout the preceding chapters, every person and situation is unique. Hopefully, as you have read through this book, there have been a few eye-opening life applications and helpful truths to aid you along your journey.

We can't deny having feelings, or emotions that dominate our thoughts when life drops out around us. So often we worry more about what others think, than what God does. Those feelings and emotions are there because we are confused, or have fear of the unknown. Life has abruptly changed and can never have the carefree routine it previously held. History confirms that strength comes from, or is a result of adversity, not compliancy.

As harsh as this next statement may sound, it's true. We don't really know who God is, until God is our only option.

Pain and disappointment happens. As humans, we want to avoid or ignore it, the normal tendency is to do something that makes us feel good, even if it is indulging in what we know is wrong. It should be no surprise that we make the most important decisions in our lives during difficult times, simply because things have changed, and we are forced to make choices to adapt. We choose either to become better by giving of self, or take the attitude of bitterness. The negative things that constantly knock you down are wearing you out; you are tired and want relief from the feeling of being stagnant or going backward.

Don't let the evil of this world overwhelm or defeat you. Remember, as a believer you are a child of the King, waiting for your faith to be sight. There is absolutely nothing this world can offer you that even comes close to the rewards of a person who pursues God. Even Jesus asked the question in Mark 8:36: "What good is it for a man to gain the whole world, yet forfeit his soul?"

The core of life is our relationship with God. If you do not know God on a personal basis, read Romans 10:9–10 or Ephesians 2:8–9; they will tell you how to have that relationship and be sealed with Christ for all of eternity.

Following is a list to inspire your thoughts, while summing up what we need to focus on to move forward after life has dealt us the undesirable:

Dwell on the positive, be thankful in all things, pray for wisdom and endurance, allow God to be in control, pray for others, take the focus off yourself; never give up hope, sing praises, pray out loud and in the name of Jesus, expect answers, seek God, read his word, forgive, don't judge, be patient, let go of bitterness and envy, seek council, control your tongue, stop comparing yourself to others, love unconditionally, and encourage others.

For those desiring to help the hurting, I give the following: Loneliness and boredom are enemies; make an effort to be a companion. Even when time has lapsed, don't forget them; the odds are they still in need of encouragement. Show genuine concern by listening, and giving opinions only when asked. The personal touch of handshakes and hugs are appreciated. Use tender words when speaking. Never make them feel they are being judged or disciplined, but rather how important and valuable they are.

One observation I have made even while writing this book, is how many different things hinge on each other, whether for the positive or the negative. I'm amazed how our emotions and personal choices influence not only our own lives, but have a lasting affect on those who are observing us.

I have had several people comment in an encouraging way to my wife and me of how they had observed our choices while dealing with the uncertainty our particular difficulty challenged us with. They also stated how it was encouraging them to make better choices.

The observation and conclusion I suspect most are trying to make concerning those dealing with life's disruptions, is what relationship that person had with Christ before, during, and after the trial. Is their relationship with God genuine or for some personal gain? They may make a decision about their own relationship with Christ, based on the example seen.

It matters not which side of the hurt you are on; you cannot remain the same if you are involved. The on-the-sidelines observer is the one who will lose the most by not gaining a friend, relationship, or personal growth. Yes, you probably will make some mistakes, but we all learn by them, and forgiveness is always possible if asked for with a truly repentant spirit.

Hopefully you have discovered by reading this book how different words and some of their meanings, personal choices, and the influence of others, have major impacts on not only you, but also those around you. My goal was to show the many different ways self gets in the way, and how we relate to each other as humans.

Once again, I will jog your memory by listing some words, and as you read through the list, try to verbally state their meanings and how it might influence an outcome from whatever side of hurt you are on.

Hurt, Mere Words, Council, Fear, Wisdom, Despair, Do's, Don'ts, Worry, Attitude, Loneliness, Compassion, Selfish, Judged, Frustrated, Avoid, Thankful, Understanding, Perspective, Confused, Tired, Valueless, Loved, Privileged, Stuff, Prayer, Action, Exposed, Relationships, Guilt, Comparison, Stagnant, Self Esteem, Relationships, Communication, Contentment, Training.

I know the list brings a lot of information to comprehend and analyze, but I also know these words can help you pinpoint where you are personally. If one or more of these words made you uncomfortable, I challenge you to figure out why, and to make any necessary adjustments in your life. We can only make adjustments and move on when we discover what we are dealing with. Seek help and understanding before making decisions that can bring lasting consequences or blessings.

Positive words and attitudes are what each of us desires to hear, or have for encouragement during the difficult times in life. Words like peace, joy, thankful, friend, loved, and caring, along with the reflective attitude that goes with them like smiles, listening ears, hugs, and giving of personal time to share the burden.

Being thankful, is not only a result of the right spirit and attitude, but encourages each of us when we come to understand all the good things we experience and how little we deserve.

If you are the hurting, suffering, discouraged, or lonely, my prayer is for this to be an encouraging start to a positive recovery. If you are the helper or encourager, I hope you may have gleaned some insight, as to why those on the other side may feel and react to negative circumstances, not only allowing you to aid them, but desiring that you do.

Hurting people want someone to physically come alongside in a nonjudgmental manner. Remember, actions speak the loudest. You may not need to say anything; just being there is encouragement. It shows the other person they are important enough for you to interrupt your personal schedule.

Idle or misinterpreted words can quickly cause the hurting person to shut you out in defense. If you come with an overbearing approach, exclaiming something like, "What you really need to do…" I guarantee it does not matter what you have to say beyond that initial statement, because they are no longer listening to you. The proper way to help is in love. Come alongside with encouragement, not by pushing your own agenda. The only thing some have left in times of tribulation is their integrity. Let them keep it; they are a person just like you.

They feel life has treated them unfairly; they are vulnerable, confused, exposed, and the emotions can run ahead of logic. Allow for these things, listen to them, let them know you care by your actions of attention and personal sacrifice of time, and maybe even personal resources. Don't avoid them or minimize their situation. Allow them the time it takes to work through the unsolicited disruption in life. Place yourself in their position, walk in their shoes. How would you want others to respond to you if it were your trial?

Things happen for a reason, good and bad. Sometimes it's because we reap what we sow. The bad things we reap because of our own actions are hard to swallow, even if we do deserve it. The best we can do at that point is to admit our shortcomings, ask for forgiveness, and then move on by learning from our mistakes and living with the consequences. We can't go back and certainly don't want to be stuck in some negative situation, if we have the ability to get beyond it. So make the best choice after seeking council; take action by actively pursuing that choice.

Another reason things come into our lives may not be because of anything we did, but to help us grow or to glorify God through it. The correct position is to willingly accept what has come our way with the right attitude, spirit, and motivation.

I have another bold statement for the hurting individual. *Transformation within you starts transformation around you.* In other words, be the one who takes the first steps to new beginnings with a confident outlook! A life of meaning is the first step to a life of contentment.

Life is about personal choices. When hurt happens, we choose to wallow in self-pity, or use it for personally learning while teaching and encouraging those around us. I never suggested it was easy or that the direction was clear. However, the outcome and ripple effect, usually are a direct result of your choices and attitude.

Probably one of the biggest issues to deal with as a hurting person is fear of the unknown. Uncertainty and lack of direction seem beyond reach when we need it the most. Not knowing what to expect or how to prepare for what is coming, creates additional stress at a difficult time.

My challenge to those desiring to help is this: If you have had an experience or similar trial, there is nobody better qualified than you to come alongside of the hurting, but only if you have the right attitude. From my own experience, I can tell you, I really appreciated those who were blunt in the aspect of what to expect. Sugar coating and watering things down does not help the hurting prepare for what is ahead. That being said nobody should be excused from being helpers just because you have not had some particular difficulty in life. God wants all of us to be what we can, to whom we can, when we can.

The greatest ability is availability. We make the choice to get involved or not. Don't miss the opportunity to serve God when he makes it possible in your life. Remember whom you are ultimately doing it for, and that God gives blessings to those who serve him with a willing heart.

Although you may be doing things to help others during their difficult time, it is very possible their struggle could help you in numerous ways too, like strengthening your faith, building a relationship, giving you purpose, keeping you accountable, and maybe even finding enjoyment or satisfaction in helping.

When the trial or difficulty seems to have ended, it hasn't. There are scars and possible changes in lifestyle that may never go away. When someone loses a loved one, the loneliness doesn't just stop. If a job loss or sickness has caused financial distress, it may take many years to dig back out. Continue to uphold or encourage those whose lives have been altered.

We all need each other at some time during life, regardless of how invincible and self sufficient we convince ourselves we are. I can't emphasize enough the principle of Matthew 7:12, which says: "So in everything, do to others what you would have them do to you."

All these words mean nothing if we can't grasp or understand how to implement them. First, we need to take a few steps back and seek council or wisdom. *Wisdom* is *the ability to understand the accumulated information we have become aware of and make sensible decisions or judgments accordingly.* Taking the time and effort to gain understanding can save heartache later. When we have compared choices, it gives a level of comfort and determination to proceed with confidence.

Although most hurts that disrupt our lives are humiliating, a word of caution needs to be mentioned. Pride in the recovery process concerning our abilities, can hinder us from maturing. Be careful your pride does not become your motivation; give credit where credit is due. The word *joy* is a good example of what our position of service needs to be. Jesus-Others-Yourself, and in that order, stands as a guide and reminder where we fit in, while we have the privilege of living and serving others for a few short years on this earth.

We all have memories of what we have done in the past. If they were negative or brought us personal feelings of failure or regret, we wish to forget them and bury them deep, hoping never to relive the feelings again. The opposite should be true as we observe, learn, and mature from the experience.

We also have positive memories to encourage us, especially those we come in contact with who have been good examples. May we have the ability to pull up those memories when we need the stamina, empowering us to press on and be the next generation to set a good example for those behind us. Pray with faith, believing and expecting answers, not necessarily for what you want, but what benefits others or glorifies your maker.

Now for those who have read this book but are not the ones hurting or experiencing some negative aspect of life at this time. Maybe you have never had to deal with anything in life that forced you to make a major change. It is also conceivable that right now you have brushed off most of what has been addressed as some over-the-top, irrational, pathetic, one-sided opinion, possibly even thinking someone needs to pull themselves up by the bootstraps and accept life as it is. They need to move on without trying to get others to feel sorry for them.

Before you draw that conclusion, I challenge you to think of one person you may know who has in the past, or is presently dealing with the most tragic situation any human has ever encountered. Then substitute yourself for that person, asking what choices you would make and how your emotions or feelings influence the outcome. At the present time, you feel secure and unsusceptible to such demise, convincing yourself because of abilities or resources that it couldn't happen to you. Yes, it can happen to you; be prepared!

Until Christ returns to set things right or you are taken home to heaven, life can and will bring trouble or hurts to everybody at some time. Our responsibility is to have the right attitude and motivation in all things, setting self aside for the glory of God.

Life is about choices. Most of us are capable of making intelligent choices. When life turns sour, you have been humiliated or things don't work the way you had planned, you will be faced with making choices. Remember, relationships matter, and whatever choices you make will affect you and those around you for a very, very long time. Consider the long-term benefits and consequences and for whom you are living. Make every day count, because you only get a certain number, and nobody gets to relive them.

We live according to what we believe is true. Faith and hope trump worry and fear every time.

There can be no better end to this book than three verses of challenge from the book of Philippians.

- Philippians 1:27 "Whatever happens, conduct yourselves in a manner worthy of the gospel of Christ."
- Philippians 4:11 "For I have learned to be content whatever the circumstance."
- Philippians 4:13 "I can do all things through him (Christ) who gives me strength."

Life is a journey of which we know not the time
Plans of achievement, our own futures will define
When life becomes senseless, remember Christ is there
Ready willing and able, your burdens to share
Be the fruit of the spirit, with love, joy, and peace
From binding sin, you will likely have great release
Peace, patience, kindness, goodness, and faith, are a taste
Of the blessings that wait for us, because of Gods grace
Gentleness and self-control, against there is no law
Our comprehension of who God is, is so very small
It takes a lifetime to learn, understand, and grow
Choosing to live for, love, and our creator know
Well done thou good and faithful servant, may be heard
From the heavenly father, if you've heeded his word
How will others remember you, what will they say?
Hopefully that you gave of self and sought God each day!

Bibliography

All definitions are from:

Microsoft Encarta College Dictionary. 1 ed. Microsoft. St. Martin's Press, 2001.